RED
DEVILS

A History of Man United's
Rogues and Villains

RICHARD KURT

PRION

Other books by Richard Kurt

United We Stood
Despatches from Old Trafford
As the Reds Go Marching On
Cantona
The Red Army Years
Don't Look Back in Anger – Growing Up With Oasis

Acknowledgements

Without the help of Andy Pollard,
creator of *You're Supposed To Be At Home*,
I'd never get anything done: thanks again Andy

Thanks as ever for all sorts to Chris Nickeas,
Peter Boyle, Tony Veys, Andy Walsh;
to Bill Campbell for his incredibly patient understanding;
to Garth Dykes for advice;
to Andrew Goodfellow and Ian Marshall

CONTENTS

First published in 1998 by
Prion Books Limited
32–34 Gordon House Road,
London NW5 1LP

A catalogue record of this book can be obtained from the British Library

ISBN 1-85375-287-8

Cover design by Vivid

Printed and bound in Great Britain
by Creative Print & Design, Wales

PHOTOGRAPH ACKNOWLEDGEMENTS FOR INSERT SECTION

All-Sport/Vandystadt p.8
Exotica Archive pp.1, 2, 3, 4, 7
Mirror Syndication International pp. 5, 6

EMPATHY
FOR THE
DEVILS

Best to start by confessing to a sleight-of-pen: technically, Manchester United weren't always the Red Devils, and perhaps it's a bit of a cheek to recast our entire history as if we were. Indeed, the irony is that the 50s decade in which we acquired – some say stole – our demonic nickname constituted the least devilish period of the United story. Never were the Reds so apparently upright, virtuous and eminently lovable as they were in the ten years before the Munich crash, a fact which made that disaster all the more grievous to both United supporters and the world at large. Nevertheless, the favoured moniker of Salford's Rugby League team duly travelled the few manors south to Old Trafford and, by the time my thirty-something generation was filling the Stretford End, the little red lucifer and his trident were firmly ensconsed upon the Club badge. One would hope that not even the plc would dare remove it now, although such considerations haven't prevented the Orwellian disappearance of the phrase "Football Club" from that same icon.

Naturally, our detractors like to point out that this acquisition of the Red Devil was a typical piece of United robbery, just as we adapt other clubs' anthems, erode their local fan bases and buy their carefully nurtured stars at their peak. But I would suggest that the Red Devil is indeed a perfect symbol of at least part of United's tradition.

Who wants to be a Linekerish goody-goody after all? The history that people enjoy reading about and even emulating is not that built upon the creations of the angels – your Cliff Richards, Doris Days and so forth – but that forged by the demonic, by the likes of Keith Richards and Marlon Brando. What that tells us about the human race I do not know, but there it is. So at United, we have cool respect and admiration for Bobby Charlton but it's Denis and George whom we red-bloodedly love. We take the rogue over the role model every time.

This book gathers up all the leading rogues, anti-heroes and downright villains who've been through Old Trafford to provide an alternative paradigm of United-ness. It's about bungs, bad fouls, baiting authority and banging barmaids rather than goals and trophies. That said, this isn't really just a collection of individual character sketches. I hope you'll see that, gene-like, common strands run through the chapters of history which together form a large part of the Club's DNA structure. It's another way of going from 1878 to 1998, except we're taking the dodgier low road. Of course it is right that the noble legends of Busby, Duncan Edwards and Johnny Carey dominate United literature but football isn't always about glory, honour and the highest callings. The Devil has some pretty good tunes too...

THE
HEATHENS

If Newton Heath play Burnley next week in their ordinary style,
it will perhaps create an extraordinary run of business for the
undertakers...

Birmingham Gazette 16 October, 1893

A typical southern softie comment of the period, though one
which would carry more import than most as it set off a train
of events which drove Newton Heath itself into a coffin. And
admittedly, there were more than mere geographic reasons to
dub United's 1890s ancestors "The Heathens". Indeed, given
that the Club had moved grounds to Clayton during the summer of '93, they were no longer technically "of the Heath"
anyway. Yet the nickname stuck, for good reason: they were
the hardest, meanest muthas in the First Division. Quaking
southerners – anyone south of Withington – felt justified in
calling them Heathens because, after 90 minutes against the
likes of George Perrins and Johnny Clements, they were convinced they'd been amongst the satanically godless. The entire
division was gutted to see the Club escape relegation at the
end of 1892/3 by winning a replayed play-off, such had been
the dread engendered by a trip to our North Road hell-hole.
To many, it had seemed entirely appropriate that 1892/3's
footballing fatality – Darwen's Joe Aspden – had been the

result of an over-the-top in-the-guts flying tackle by James Brown, playing for the Devil's own side Newton Heath. No one liked us and we didn't care: throughout 1893/4, our infamy continued to grow even faster than our debts.

Therein lay a consolation for the critics – Heath were poor and a bit crap as well as dirty, and were thus unlikely to survive for long in the increasingly Mammon-worshipping top flight. Years of being sucked dry by North Road landlords left the Club staggering from one financial crisis to another, never able to import the very best talent which continued to flock to the likes of Sunderland and Aston Villa. Even when Heath tried to play cultured football, the grotesque surface at North Road sabotaged their efforts. If you thought the Old Trafford pitch was a bit of a disgrace in 1991, it was a croquet lawn compared to the assault course-cum-minefield that was North Road. Used for every human leisure activity known to Victorian man, and constructed from every unsuitable substance in the earth's crust, the pitch was only fit for hacking and, perhaps, artillery practice. Unsurprisingly, Heath developed a style which even then was dubbed "kick and rush", essentially involving hoofed airborne balls pursued by packs of fearsome, slightly rabid forwards – and God have mercy on the souls of any stupid or brave fullback who stood his ground.

Football, to put it mildly, was a tad more physical back then. Goalkeepers, for example, were not the puffy union of protected species they are today, whereby any striker who farts in their general direction is sent off for aggressive conduct. Especially before 1894, goalies were fair game for massed assault (innocently known as "charging"), with the location of the ball often immaterial. Heath, in their defence, would often point out that several other Northern sides specialised in kick 'n' rush and the physical side of the game; hadn't even southern ponces Wolves just won the FA Cup in similar fashion? All true, of course: but no-one took quite such pleasure as Heath in sizing up oppo goalies and calculating how many burly six-foot Scottish forwards it would take to steamroller him and his shattered teeth into his own net.

It had been hoped that the move to Clayton's Bank Street stadium would benefit both Heath and their quivering opposition alike. For the Club, there was the promise of decent grass instead of green clay and a cheap rent. Visitors appreciated the surface and the prospect of a safer environment generally. Local fans, who'd developed their own reputation for drunken carousing and fisticuffs, were reckoned to be unlikely to trek the three miles to the new venue, thus allowing visitors to breathe more easily amidst a better class (*sic*) of customer. But after a couple of weeks of supporter grumbling, the old lads were soon making the journey to watch the Shirts once again, and Bank Street became as unwelcome an awayday as North Road had ever been. Indeed, it acquired its own unique notoriety thanks to a tactical deployment of the adjacent chemical works of which Saddam Hussein would've been proud. The factory emitted the vilest gaseous stench in Manchester, easily trouncing the legendary rendering plant in north Manchester which had reputedly turned most of the locals vegetarian. Our lads became quickly accustomed to the all-pervading choke whereas the opposition would stagger around helplessly on arrival, no doubt wishing there was some Victorian version of UNSCOM available to close down what was clearly a violation of civilised warfare codes. When a couple of journalists noticed that the stink seemed to become even worse when Heath were losing – i.e. midway through every game – a myth developed that local fans monitoring the games from inside the plant were purposely piling on extra noxious compounds of chlorine and nitrogen whenever the opposition scored. It tells you something about the wretched quality of the team that even with such help, we still only won five of our 15 home games. We would end the season relegated, with Liverpool beating us in the playoffs to take our place. Insofar as the respiratory tracts of an entire generation of first division footballers were saved – not to mention all the limbs that would now remain unbroken – it constituted a rare example of Scousers doing something for the benefit of the game as a whole. And as few fans had the cars from which hubcaps could be nicked, it's no exaggeration to state that the entire division, fans and players alike, were delighted to witness our demise and the ascent of the Liverpudlians. They wouldn't be seeing the Heathens again; their next trip to Bank Street would be to play Manchester United. For during 1893/4, Newton Heath would allow their devilish attitude to take them over the edge, into an abyss of destitution and bankruptcy.

That Heath remained a viable concern for so long was largely due to the brilliant juggling of the legendary A H Albut, the Club secretary acquired from Aston Villa. In an era of showmen and carnival personalities, Albut was a natural – sharp-witted, a dab hand with creative accounting and a PR's dream who loved dealing with the press and getting involved in their backpage capers. His favoured habitat was back-to-the-wall in a tight corner, all the better for him to pull off a somersaulting leap over his adversaries' heads. Council cut off all the gas and leccy? Albut would rustle up fifty lights out of beer bottles and candles in a jiffy. Accounts looking like they've got scarlet fever? A couple of 'tax-efficient' brown envelope deals and solvency appears from nowhere. Fancy a player who's under contract to a club who won't let him go? Engineer a pop-press photo-stunt which so embarrasses the player's club that they feel honour-bound to sell him – then step in to sign him at half the value.

A bit of nous and a sense of adventure could get you a long way in those days, when Britain was still nowhere near resembling a meritocracy and whose administration was often in the hands of minor public school bumblers. (Like United still are today, funnily enough.) Albut shimmied and swerved his way around innumerable obstacles with sometimes questionable legality, dragging the ailing patient of a Club behind him. But he had ideals too. He grew to love the Club, seeing his mission as more than just a job, and he spotted early on that the growth of professionalism threatened to divide players from their fans. Typical of him was the idea of a Newton Heath Social Club, providing cheap drinks and an ambience wherein players and fans could mix together on equal terms, play snooker and generally bind the Club's community together. (Sadly, as is always the case with such 'brotherhood of man' ventures in Manchester, it came to a Hacienda-style end: too many local scallies causing trouble and too many patrons nicking club property at the rate of thirty snooker cues per month.) Above all, it was Albut's job to keep the players happy during an era in which much of the wage bill was paid in "divvies" – the surplus of the gate receipts after running expenses, split 11 ways – and to which boot deals and hair-gel contracts appeared as futuristically implausible as losing the Empire. How much of his fateful decision to sue a newspaper for libelling the team was down to the desire to back his players' reputations? One would hope, knowing the man's record, that this was the key factor rather than some silly notion of wounded civic pride on the Football Club company's behalf. Much better to go down blazing as a *fin-de-siècle* adventurer backing his troops than as a stuffy tight-arsed Victorian prig.

Albut would've been entirely justified in blaming the next decade's trauma on the blithering imbecile who reffed Heath's visit to Derby on 7 October 1893. The team hadn't started the season too badly – a couple of wins gave them mid-table security and the chemical warfare at Bank Street was functioning nicely. But in a hack-fest free-for-all in the Midlands, which ended in a 2-0 defeat, Newton Heath's lads were faced with a situation akin to that of a Red in an unattended continental bar. Derby's boys were up for it, the ref seemed unable or unwilling to take control and the linesmen spent most of the match looking up into the clouds muttering "nothing to do with me, Guv". The Heathens reverted to nature and got stuck in to frightening effect, reprising all the old tunes from 92/3 such as "Play The Knee, Not The Ball", "You're Going Home In A St. John's Horse And Cart" and "Nutmeg Me Again, If You Want Me To Make You Look Like John Merrick". The FA, stunned by match reports containing casualty details last seen in the Crimea, felt forced to launch an inquiry: three Heathens, including specialist cropper John Clements, would eventually be suspended for a fortnight even though they'd only been booked. The referee was banned from officiating for the rest of the season for being crap at his job, another old-time practice that we don't see enough of these days. The press dusted off all the old Heathen cliches from '92/3 and rubbed their hands in glee, ready for the Bank Street encounter against West Brom.

Newton Heath beat West Brom 4-1; in purely footballing terms, it was their best performance of the early 90s. And Heath always did have a couple of good players, characters who could put a tenner on the gate. Men such as the exciting Jack Peden, the first Irishman to play in the English League, a local Belfast Boy hero at outside-left 70 years before his rather more famous successor. Or Brummie Alfie Farman, a quiet and clever operator who possessed the most outrageously lethal long-range shot in football with which he once scored from the touchline thirty-five yards out. Or Bob Donaldson, a Scottish targetman with a big reputation who could've named his price when joining Heath but refused to take more than his team-mates were earning.

But you were never far away from the darker flipside; in Donaldson, for example, lurked a goalie-hating beast of whom a team-mate said, "When Bob goes up in the box, everything else has to go down." (Any photo of Bob invariably showed him heading the ball home whilst some poor sap in green is prostrate on the floor, trying to remember where he is and why his nose is in his mouth.) Tommy Fitzsimmons was a decent enough Scottish forward but with a mean streak as wide as his carnivalesque moustache; Georgie Perrins was a young Brummie rightback with the fatal combination of troublesome mouth, boot and fist. John Clements at left back was simply hard, who used his speed across the turf mainly in order to achieve a better fouls-per-minute ratio. Almost always under treatment, he once estimated that 90 per cent of his injuries resulted from his own fouls. That day against West Brom, all these Heathens were stars...of a sort.

At first, there was little comment about the game's more physical aspects, with most papers content to praise Heath for their all-out attacking style. But on Monday 16 October, the *Birmingham Gazette* ran an astringent match report, stuffed full of the provincial bias and wounded pride that these days would be more readily associated with fanzines. The writer, one William Jephcott, ended his peroration with that opening undertakers jibe, but only after running through a catalogue of indignant accusations. He'd alleged that a ruck of Heathens deliberately booted West Brom's keeper whilst he was on the ground after the ball had gone in for the opening goal; that Georgie Perrins had virtually drop-kicked Geddes in the back, leaving "a lump the size of a duck egg" which later forced him out of the game; that Jack Peden had perpetrated a whole series of "dirty tricks", apparently with CIA-like stealth; that the Baggies' Horton had been "brutally kicked in the head" and that in general Heath's contribution had "not been football but simple brutality". He called on the FA to investigate just as it had done after the Battle of Derby and declared that "for the good of the game", Heath should be severely sanctioned.

And there, with an outburst of parochial bluster, the matter would have rested, had not some mischievious soul clipped the Brummie's fulminations and mailed it to Bank Street. Within days, the matter would be brought to the Mancunian public's attention, and from there to the national agenda as football's Legal Match of the Decade. Newton Heath's red devil entrails would be exposed for the nation's newspaper readers to pick over, sprinkled with *schadenfreude*: at last, would the Bank Street Beasts be getting their come-uppance?

Back in 1893, Manchester's greatest gift to the world of journalism, the *Guardian*, still resided in its birthplace. Quick to pick up on the rumblings of discontent from Newton Heath's directors about the *Gazette*'s attack, they immediately ran stories about the Bank Street Battle but concluded editorially that the Club needed to lighten up and chill out. But Albut had already swung into retaliatory action, weakened perhaps by his personal lust for newsprint action: he had, remarkably, persuaded J R Strawson, the match referee, to write to the *Guardian* letters page to debunk the Brummie's allegations. In an unprecedented outburst, the ref duly raged against the "abominable scurrility" of the charges, claiming that "more untruthful and groundless accusations were never made against any club" and that the writer in question had an "unhealthy imagination produced by gross partisanship". Albut would have read the missive with glee – what a potential witness! Down in Brum, they muttered a more cynical line; what else could a blind or weak ref who felt guilty at missing so much foul play do but pretend it never happened? After all, he didn't want to end up like the chump in the black at Derby, did he?

Strawson conceded that Reader, the Brom keeper, had been kicked, but that it had been accidental. And yes, Geddes had been injured but he hadn't even appealed for a foul. In a rousing finale, worthy of any Heath season ticket holder, he proclaimed that in fourteen years he'd "never had a pleasanter afternoon's refereeing", surely the only time in history such a verdict had ever been reached by an official on duty at Bank Street. As a coda, seemingly designed to shove enraged Baggies into apoplexy, Strawson even claimed that several Brom players had approached him after the game to pass on their appreciation of the fair play exhibited by Heath. You can imagine the effect this had down at Albion, where the club secretary already had seven players who'd volunteered to testify in court that The Heathens were, well, heathens. So when Newton Heath filed their writ against the *Gazette*, there was no way Albion were going to back out of a rematch or pressure the paper to settle out of court. The prospect of giving the likes of Perrins and Peden a good seeing-to in the witness box was simply too irresistible.

By the time the case came up before Justice Day in Manchester's court in March, Newton Heath's directors could be forgiven for feeling rather less cocky than they did when Albut set the legal wheels in motion. The team was in disarray, rooted to the foot of the division after an appalling sequence of 11 straight losses, unable to play, kick or poison their way out of the mire. Sections of the media had whipped up a heady brew in anticipation of the ground-breaking trial as they understandably sought to establish their journalistic rights to criticise football clubs in the public interest. Heath had their support too, from within the game at least. The extraordinary growth of professional football over the previous five years had elevated the top clubs and their officials into prominent positions in the community. An entire class of grocers, *petit bourgeois* businessmen and municipal stuffed shirts had found themselves in charge of thriving concerns with important civic and commercial reputations to maintain; this almost masonic band of football people saw the press vultures as potentially troublesome enemies and consequently looked forward to seeing the upstart Jephcott slapped down by Britain's vicious defamation laws, *pour encourager les autres*.

Yet despite the import of the case, the main sound to be heard from the courthouse over the two days of hearings was laughter, as a series of no-nonsense meatheads took to the witness stand to prick the pomposity of the barristers, under the benevolent and slightly naughty aegis of Justice Day. A forerunner of *Private Eye*'s Justice Cocklecarrot, Day revelled in the case's notoriety and played upon the assembled wigs' sycophancy by cracking as many lame one-liners as possible. But then, being faced with a parade of ridiculously partisan witnesses, half of whom were clearly lying their arses off, a sense of humour was probably essential. His eventual judgment had a cunning Solomonesque quality to it which suggested he was never as out of touch as he claimed to be; there was to be no Victorian equivalent of "Who Is Gazza?", for example.

Newton Heath's squad, led by briefs Shee and Bradbury, were on home turf once again, a great psychological advantage over QC Gully and his Baggie followers who huddled together in court like a team out for a dangerous awayday, wondering where the escort was. And Shee had two great batons with which to beat his opponents: the allegedly defamatory article, in bold black and white, which would scupper the *Gazette* unless they could prove it to be true, and the ref as a plaintiff witness which could not fail to impress the judge and jury. A pre-match bonus too: the defence's deployment of the Dalglish Gambit ("We're not playing on these terms, it's not fair, where's my bottle" etc.) also failed when the judge confirmed that even if Heath hadn't lost money as a result of the article, they were still entitled to sue for damages. Albut rubbed his hands – a result here, and they'd have seen the last of the Council's utility disconnection squad.

Jephcott, brimming with indignant zeal, repeated his article from the stand, chucking in for extra effect the allegations that it was Tommy Fitzsimmons who'd booted Brom's keeper Reader on the deck and that Johnny Clements had "charged" Barton viciously more than once. (In a Victorian context, "charge" didn't mean shoulder-to-shoulder, more a headfirst steamrollering.) One or two on the home bench squirmed a little, realising the dangers inherent in court actions – that witnessses might start lobbing up new charges with no fear of subsequent legal sanction. But Jephcott could be easily neutralised as a partisan hack with a track record of Baggie-prop. Less comfortable was the sight of four or five West Brom players warming up to take to the field. Would the jury realise how unusual it was for 'fellow pros' to testify against each other? What would they infer from that? And what if the witnesses – gulp – started to elaborate on what they knew of Newton Heath players' true natures from experience? One or two of our lads didn't exactly have clean charge sheets...

Sure enough, every Baggie added a little morsel to the *smörgåsbord* of vileness until the jury's plate groaned under the weight. Horton, for example, not only confirmed he'd been booted in the skull but added that he'd been kneed in the unmentionables by a "grinning" Heathen. (Cue sniggers from the press box.) Geddes, rather pathetically, claimed that the kick he received in the back was so bad that he'd had to have oil rubbed into it, which hardly impressed observers used to seeing exposed tibia and severed fingertips at Bank Street. But rather damningly, he revealed that his alleged assailant Georgie Perrins had 'form' with him: when the clubs had met in September, he'd accidentally kicked Perrins in the eye, who promptly 'went postal' and chased him around the pitch. At full-time, Perrins had cornered him and promised, "I'll give you one for that", and he didn't mean a blowjob. It had been a clever move by the defence. Now the jury had been alerted to Heath's 'previous' and the suggestion that they'd all been acting in character. The rumpus at Derby was bound to come up too; how could they expect the jury to remain unprejudiced if the entire history of the Heathens' naughtiness was to emerge?

On it went: the Brom captain, almost squeaking with outrage, emphasised that the goalie had been booted when the ball was already in the net; that Peden had spent the entire 90 minutes hacking; and that three or four others did nothing but charge and foul. Another claimed it had been "the roughest game of all time" and that a raving John Clements had jumped onto his back as he tried to dribble round him. More press sniggers: Mad John was notorious for his, um, 'specialised' tackling techniques. Tom Perry gave a second-by-second account of a Peden classic – the full-speed over-the-top 'tackle' that is aimed just below the knee for maximum incapacity – before dryly adding that he'd had three opportunities to study this technique from the receiving end. Finally, the goalkeeper Reader backed every other West Brom witness's account, before landing the ref right in the shit: Reader claimed the players had indeed gone to the ref after the match, but to complain, not to applaud. The ref had replied that if they'd felt they'd been fouled, they should've appealed straight away – which in Reader's case would've been tricky as he'd had his face embedded in the mud. And there was an added *frisson* around the court as a snippet of hearsay was repeated: a Newton Heath cry directed at the Baggie dressing room afterwards of "that's how we'll be sorting out Burnley next week, an' all." With the grisly details of the skirmish at Derby duly emerging too, it made for a grim afternoon for Newton Heath.

Still, secretary Albut was confident as ever in his own ability; he'd surely charm and dazzle his way through from the stand and turn the case around. Unfortunately, someone with even better press contacts than his had been busy, and had unearthed a rather juicy soundbite some hack had heard Albut emit at a sportsman's dinner. "We have a clever way of succeeding with rough conduct," Albut allegedly quipped, "we do it when the ref's not looking." Hoots and hollers filled the courtroom. The judge, trying hard not to giggle, intervened to clarify: "Mr. Albut, do you confirm you made such a remark?" Albut, for once in a corner too tight even for him,

replied, "Well, it was a very merry dinner, m'lud." More guf-
faws. Justice Day: "Are you saying you were too drunk to
remember?" Albut, brilliantly: "Perhaps I was too drunk to
know if I was too drunk to remember?" (Court collapses and
adjourns.)

The Heathens' case continued to teeter on the brink of outright farce all day as Fitzsimmons, Perrins and Peden all came
forward to testify. To a man, they all stuck to their guns, offering grunting monosyllabic replies where possible, leavened by
the occasional pearler. Tommy, accused directly of kicking
Horton in the head, parried superbly with a deadpan
response: "Well, I'd need to lift my leg rather high for that,
wouldn't I?" Perrins, denying all suggestions of revenge as a
motive for booting Geddes, cleverly turned the tables on the
wimpy Baggie by alleging that he'd twice before seen Geddes
flounce off football fields with minor injuries. In an era when
indestructible manliness was the muscular Christian's prime
virtue, this was a smart trick for the jury's benefit. And the
judge had admitted to being a footballer as a youngster; surely he would recognise that no 'real man' leaves a football field
during play unless his limb count falls below three?

Only Peden got into any serious difficulty when the
defence QC brought up his charge sheet. He managed to
escape the accusation that he'd caused opponents to suffer
broken legs in the past but he had to admit that he'd been suspended for injuring a player by kicking him in the stomach.
The classic excuse? "I mistook his stomach for the ball because
I was temporarily blinded by the sun." Yes, an easy mistake to
make and one which surely demanded sympathy rather than
two minutes of courtroom tittering...

So it had boiled down to that nastiest of legal dilemmas –
one word against another. And to be honest, Newton Heath's

bon mots looked slightly less unblemished than West Brom's. But Shee had a trump up his sleeve; he could come to the jury's rescue by offering more 'independent' witnesses to settle the deadlock, as if it were a judicial penalty shoot-out. Distinguished journalist E H Davies, a cheerful bouncy fellow who just happened to do the odd bit of work for Mancunian papers, breezily declared from the box that it had been a top match, full of skill, and that the *Gazette*'s comments had been "whimsical and absurd". In a *tour de force* performance, he spun the guns around to face the *Gazette* once more: "In Manchester, London and Liverpool, we enjoy an honest and impartial local press. But in four-fifths of the rest of the country, we do not – and Birmingham is among the worst offenders." Here was a jury-swinging witness, a gentleman of the press prepared to break ranks and testify against a comrade, despite the great issues of state in play. The door was now open for Shee to place the ball on the spot for his next witness to strike home for victory.

What archetype in Victorian Britain commanded more immediate respect than any other? The local Reverend, purveyor of the religion and civilization which our Empire sought to propagate throughout the world. In that era before the *News of the World* began to specialise in defrocking pulpit paedophiles and altar adulterers, no upright citizen would believe a vicar capable of lying in God's witness box. The Rev. Reid (of Miles Platting, it should be admitted) came out and played a blinder. Not only did he testify that it had been a jolly super contest with nothing ungodly or untoward, it had actually been "a tad too tame"! Brilliantly, he cited his female companion (hmm...maybe the *NOTW* missed something here) who had declared that she had been disappointed not to have seen more of the hard play she had expected after the previous weekend's Derby match. This, of course, was hearsay, and should've been inadmissable – but no brief was going to accuse a vicar of breaking the false witness Commandment in Victorian England. It was later muttered that the Rev. was a Newton Heath home-and-away fanatic and had probably done a deal with God so that he could do his duty by his team but at that moment he saved the Heath from defeat and instant bankruptcy. The jury promptly found for the plaintiffs, after a judge's direction that stressed the importance of the independent witnesses' accounts and during which he rather rogueishly observed that football crowds liked it rough anyway.

Albut and the directors celebrated as the players revelled in their 'vindication' but the judge had a final, off-the-ball assault of his own in mind. He awarded Newton Heath damages of "the smallest coin of the realm" – one farthing, a quarter of an old penny, an amount that buys bugger all no matter what century you're in. Albut was horrified, having bargained for hundreds of pounds for his libel jackpot. Worse was to come: each side would have to pay their own costs, rather than the norm of the losers paying both sides'. Instead of being the modern equivalent of twenty grand up, Newton Heath were about ten down. Some victory: like winning a Coca-Cola Cup match but losing ten players to injury. For a club on daily waking terms with near insolvency and with no prospect of playing success, it constituted a devastating blow; Newton Heath would spend the next eight years in a doomed struggle for survival.

So Justice Day, despite his hammery and feigned ignorance, truly had known the score after all. These libel judgments where costs are split and awards negligible are quite a common feature in high profile cases; you may remember a couple from recent years involving newspaper martinets. It is the Establishment's way of telling all parties that they've been silly billies, that the case should've been settled and never brought to court. And it gives an extra slap to the 'winners', as if to say, "We've got your number, lads." Newton Heath had won in court with the equivalent of a very dodgy last minute penalty and the judge knew it. The jury's verdict, correct in an evidential sense, had nonetheless seemed perverse set against the bigger picture of infamous Heathens trying to kick and gas their opponents to destruction. Years of ill-repute had caught up with them; and as the instigators of this final act, they only had themselves to blame. Like a Victorian OJ Simpson, they would wander through the remaining wilderness years technically innocent, but barred from every decent establishment in the country for bearing the stench of guilt.

Still, they would continue to frequent the not-so-decent locales of the Second Division for a few years yet, as miserable an environment then as now, where they would be reunited with local neighbours Ardwick. Or, to be precise about their new high-falutin' nomenclature, Manchester City. At least they could give those urchins a couple of good kickings in derby matches, which they duly did in 1894/5. But City would soon be on the way up, threatening to leave the Heath behind as Manchester's poor relations. And their deadliest weapon, coveted by every club in the land as well as ours, would be the Welsh Wizard they signed in that summer of '94 – Billy Meredith. But in time, the last of Hell's Heathens would give way to the first great Red Devil.

THE
OUTCASTS

Billy Meredith was that rarity, a player and man whose contribution was so enormous that he helped define what the very words "Manchester United" mean. Arguably, there's only been three since – Duncan Edwards, George Best and Eric Cantona – and it's no accident that three of this supreme quartet are as much remembered for their rebel hearts as for their footballing ability. It's easy to forget these days, as United's size and dominance makes them appear to be the exemplars of football's Establishment, that this was always an outsiders' club, whose progress has been marked by moments of defiance, innovation and vision which separated us from both other clubs and from contemporary orthodoxy. For example: defying the FA to enter the European Cup in 1956; being the first club to step up to back players' rights, as we'll see below; challenging 70s conformity by producing an all-out attacking team which played with saintly cleanliness; and turning their backs to the market to build a club upon youth in the 50s and 90s. At all these junctures, wise men told

United they were fools, but the rebels persisted and eventually triumphed.

Back in 1902, when Newton Heath expired and Manchester United rose in its place, that tradition was yet to be forged. Meredith, an unstoppable Welsh wing wizard who scored 200 goals and made another 400 in his vast career, was at City, and if anyone was at the cutting edge of the game, it was the then Hyde Road outfit and their resident superstar. United's first 1902/03 season saw us finish a respectable 5th in Division Two – but City won promotion, and within twelve months would be clinching the FA Cup at Crystal Palace with a Meredith goal. City took 20,000 down to London and returned to mount this town's first, great welcome-home parade for a victorious team. (A tradition almost solely carried on since by United, of course.) The press marvelled at the turn-out but in particular at the extraordinary public fervour in the working-class districts exhibited towards Meredith himself. Their words fumbled towards what we can now see clearly in hindsight – Meredith was football's first genuine superstar, a household name and working-class hero.

That he was the best player in Britain was blindingly obvious even then – and most would accept that we produced no finer until well after the Second World War – but there was more to his status than that. He had star quality, a fascinating character and unique individuality that stood out in a sea of humble, deferential wage-serfs. In an increasingly visual age, as the press became more pictorial and moving pictures arrived, he looked the part too: piercing eyes, chiselled features, the trademark toothpick between his lips creating as cool an impression as Clint's cheroots fifty years later. Business flocked to offer him endorsement deals, newspaper columns, personal appearance fees: he blew away the

Victorian ideal of the 'gentleman amateur' who should sub-
sume his individuality into a public-school ethos of collectivism.
He grabbed the opportunities that came his way to make himself a national figure, and had the worthiest of underlying
motives – he intended to change the game forever. His was
not the indulgent, purpose-less self-mythologising of today's
football stars but, more in the tradition repopularised by later
Reds Charlie Mitten and Cantona, photogenic rebellion with
a cause. If there had existed Edwardian 'teenagers' in the
modern sense, the posters on their walls where Jimmy Dean
would later take his place would have featured Meredith.
Brilliant, cool, dangerous, dark-edged: he'd have been the 90s
marketeers' dream.

The parallels with Cantona continue: both were fastidious
trainers and curators of their own physiques, refusing to
indulge in the hedonism of their colleagues; both battled long
and hard with their consciences in the early days about the
very morality of taking money for partaking in sporting art;
both, once they'd decided to define themselves as 'profession-
als', then determined ruthlessly to extract their just rewards,
both for themselves and for their colleagues. Thus it is no surprise that both would at one point find themselves trying, and
failing, to drag their fellow pros forward to the next evolu-
tionary stage of unionisation and power-sharing.

I said the Manchester City of the early 1900s were cutting
edge not just because their first team played unusually attractive football and contained three or four of the country's most
entertaining players; their management was equally innova-
tive in the field of distributing brown paper bags. City, in
what proved to be typically cack-handed fashion, were leading
the way in bribery and corruption, or so the 'gentlemen' of the
FA contended. Essentially, they stuck to paying the £4

weekly maximum to their players as far as the books were concerned, whilst developing a fabulously elaborate system of under-the-counter bonuses, bungs, 'drinks' and other assorted Revenue-avoiding devices. Virtually every club was at it, especially the Northern giants, and the Victorian relics at the FA knew it – City were simply reputed to be more blatant and generous than most. One player at City was actually earning almost double the maximum wage; the sheer amount of fiddled money sloshing around meant that detection would eventually be unavoidable. Some City directors were banned and fined for such offences in 1904, but the players escaped from what was basically a warning fusillade. Next time, the FA determined, they'd get the culprits they wanted. And in that category of targets, they ranked Meredith above all.

Billy had simply become the biggest pain in the arse to the footballing establishment they'd ever known. In virtually every column, interview and article that he was involved in during that decade, Billy would seize the chance to put the economic, political and moral case for player power. Quite simply, the football market was grotesquely rigged: the maximum wage and complete contract-slavery to which players were forced to submit made football the last bastion of medieval feudalism. And where was all the money from the 40,000-plus crowds going, as it clearly went nowhere near either the players' pockets or stadium redevelopments? Hyde Road, for example, was in permanent need of renovation and repair, and most other so-called leading grounds were death-traps. The FA remained supremely unconcerned by such matters, and above all adamant that a footballer could not be treated as other employees. All over Edwardian England, workers were becoming relatively liberated, joining unions, renegotiating deals, replacing the indignity of quasi-serfdom with the dignity of citizen's labour. Not so in football: the greatest cash-generating leisure industry in England would continue to be run as if a 14th-century nobleman's plaything. It was a joke, and one that Billy delighted in retelling as often as possible to anyone who'd listen. The whole system, to him, was riddled with classic English hypocrisy, full of blind eyes, turned backs and mislabelled expenses.

The sensational showdown between Meredith's club and the FA duly arrived in 1905. What began as an inquiry into on-field violence at two City matches against Villa and Everton spiralled out of control, as dark forces manipulated witnesses and processes behind closed doors to get the kind of indictments they really wanted. The evening papers on 5 August reported the most incredible allegation domestic football had ever seen – that the nation's star player Billy Meredith had offered a £10 bribe to Aston Villa's Alec Leake to throw the City–Villa match, the equivalent of three weeks' wages to the Villain. Further allegations cascaded in its wake, mostly concerning the rampant irregularities in City's payments to players: one by one, players and officials crumbled at the knees of the FA to confess to the contents of their brown envelopes, hoping that their pleas would induce mercy. The inquiry had fulfilled the authorities' every goal – they'd smeared their Public Enemy Number One and they'd been given the opportunity to eradicate at Manchester City what they saw as a hotbed of anti-establishment practices. Both Meredith and City weren't only troublesome in themselves – they'd both been agitating nationwide to gather support for modernisation and justice. Meredith was on the verge of unionising his fellow players, whilst City had succeeded in forming an *ad hoc* alliance with other leading Northern clubs to change football's entire regulatory framework. By destroying both Billy and City, the FA and the ruling class which supported it might succeed in postponing their own day of reckoning for decades to come. Meredith got an immediate eight-month ban, even though it was largely believed that the bribery charge had been the result of a jokey misunderstanding during pre-match banter. City, as a Club, were all but demolished: directors were disbarred for life and virtually the entire playing staff given lengthy bans and ordered never to play for City again. How modern Blues must wish for some of that treatment today, hey?

A lesser man might have been ruined, or at least would have sought retreat and sanctuary. Meredith refused to be bowed. He remained as publicly vociferous as ever: damning the FA and the Club who had probably betrayed him behind the scenes; proselytising for his proposed Union. Billy made it clear from the outset – any hope the FA had that he might retire was forlorn. The minute his suspension was up, he'd be back on the field; after all, he was still only 30 and at the peak of his powers. Somehow Meredith was strong enough to shrug off the Leake allegations as though they were nothing more bothersome or shameful than a booking. Whilst the press divided between Establishement and modernisers, spending the best part of 18 months chucking pro- and anti-Meredith broadsides at each other, Billy kept training, ready for the day he'd return to make his enemies choke.

One afternoon in 1906 at the Queen's Hotel in Manchester, a handful of journalists witnessed the greatest piece of business ever conducted by Manchester United Football Club. City, forced by the FA to offload all seventeen of their indicted players, held a footballers' cattle-market, at which United snapped up the prize bulls of Meredith and three key team-mates – Turnbull, Burgess and Bannister. It is no exaggeration to claim that without that draconian FA mandate and the resultant knock-down auction, the name of Manchester United might today be no more world-famous than that of Stockport County or Oldham Athletic; without that stroke of luck, we could easily have become a small-time satellite forever circling around the sun of Manchester City. Instead, we added four crucial players to a team which within six months would be touted as Britain's finest; we established for the first time the classic United playing tradition which has bewitched football supporters ever since; and the material success they helped to accrue enabled the Club to build Old Trafford, declared to be the world's finest stadium upon its completion in 1910. And, of course, we knocked City out of the ring for years to come just at the moment when they were promising to cement their position as Manchester's main club for eternity. United's pre-war triumphs (two league titles and an FA Cup victory) built up enough credit and support to ensure that we could endure the drought of the 20s and 30s without surrendering our territorial claim on Manchester's footballing soul. All that was achieved on the back of City's own slice of notorious devilry, with players they'd cultivated for years. No wonder the Blues tend to bitterness – it's clearly an ancestral inheritance.

Meredith and the favourite cronies he brought to United with him were as tight a firm of lads as any in Manchester, and no-one was closer to Billy as player, mate and fellow battler than Alex "Sandy" Turnbull. On the field, they dovetailed as winger/inside-forward more neatly than any combination seen in football until that point: no sight was more familiar at Hyde Road than Sandy leaping to head home a pinpoint Meredith cross. An unusually clever player, in the stereotypical 'canny Scot' tradition, Turnbull was a nightmare to mark, disappearing when other players were getting stuck into frantic hurly-burly, then suddenly re-emerging with devastating cunning to thump the ball home or provide the killer lay-off. Like Jimmy Greenhoff decades later, he was regarded as the best uncapped player in Britain; unlike Jimmy, he also bore a reputation for devilish high jinks off the field, the widest swear-word vocabulary in town and a temper better suited to the days of the Heathens. If you messed with him, you got punished: it was as simple as that. It had been one of Sandy's escapades that had eventually led to the suspension of all those City players, for the investigation had begun as merely an inquiry into the on-field violence that occurred during 1905's Villa–City match. As City trailed 3-1 and Sandy grew increasingly frustrated, Villa's Alec Leake made the mistake of chucking some mud at him in retaliation for a typically bone-crunching challenge. In a trice, Sandy laid into him, landing two cracking hooks before contemptuously waving the V's at Leake whilst team-mates restrained him. As the Brummie crowd went bananas at full-time, racing outside to give the City bus a stoning, Turnbull got dragged out of the players'-tunnel and given a good kicking in the Villa dressing room. Only massive police reinforcements stopped a riot in the streets around the ground, and for days afterwards the local papers of Birmingham and Manchester refought their battle of 1895 as they tried to outdo each other in hurling lurid accusations. Sandy eventually received a month's ban, whilst his co-accused Leake got off scot-free, but by that stage of the inquiry the nation's attention was elsewhere as the press went ballistic over the bribery allegations.

Sandy was as stalwart a defender of players' rights as the rest of Meredith's crowd. This translated two ways – he played a major, even heroic, part in the struggle over the Union in 1909, but was also more heavily implicated than most in the illegal payments scandal that destroyed Manchester City. Like most of his contemporaries, he saw himself as a rebel warrior and an exploited slave, fully entitled to take what he could get from an absurdly old-fashioned and class-ridden game. So he'd had no compunction back in 1902 when he blatantly broke his word by joining City instead of Bolton, with whom he'd previously agreed terms; nor did he ever express regret over the shenanigans that had occurred at City; nor would he be able to restrain himself from going too far in the last, fateful scandal of 1915. His attitude, common amongst the increasingly militant working classes of Edwardian England, was to say "Fuck 'em – let's take what should be ours anyway." All that Victorian bullshit of gentlemen and amateurs playing for honour was dead – the 1900s were radical times, catalysed by the New Liberal agenda, the growth of the ILP and the epic legal struggles of the trades unions. Amongst players of a certain outlook and character, tampering with the supposed purity of the game was acceptable, even necessary. If the FA wouldn't grant economic and political justice to the players, then they were prepared to grab some, vigilante-style, for themelves.

Imported firebrands such as Turnbull and Meredith found their spiritual home at United, at least in terms of political morality. Their new captain Charlie Roberts was not only a born leader whose men would follow him anywhere but a fellow activist – he'd tried to launch a players' union in 1903 himself. (The FA had missed a trick here; if they could only have seen what potential there was for trouble at United once Roberts and Co. got together, they would surely have added a rider to the 1906 auction preventing any player sales to United.) Too late: in the middle of United's title season, they took the lead in launching an heroic breakout. Together with players from fourteen other clubs, they founded the new Players' Union in Manchester on 2 December 1907 with three simple demands – an end to wage restraint, the introduction of freedom of contract, and the end of the FA's *de facto* legal immunity which prevented players going to court to settle disputes. These were fundamental human rights of the kind being granted to all workers in the land, bar football's. And Manchester United as a club stepped forward at this critical moment to offer moral and tangible support, sending a message to every other club that the time had come to abandon the brown envelope underworld and take on the FA's primadonnas. Club chairman J J Davies was to be the Union's president – there could be no greater indication of United's collective rebellion.

Panic and anger blazed through the footballing establishment. What the hell were these mad Mancs playing at? City had caused enough trouble already but at least they'd been stupid enough to do it furtively; now here were United going above board and openly calling for nationwide support. One FA Council member, ranting against the new upstarts for their "contemptible claptrap", rather gave the game away by characterising this new struggle as one that was between "masters and servants". In one clipped phrase, he encapsulated the absurd feudalism of football and engendered even more support within the game for the 'serfs' at United. Football's governing bodies, as the rest of the century has confirmed, never look more ridiculous than when they set their faces against economic and political reality, trying to stem the power of free market forces like King Canutes in blazers.

Meredith's zeal and appetite for battle was something to behold. He'd only just come through 18 months of constant controversy and legal action at City; now, after a ten-month break, he was back in the saddle for a further 18 months of bitter fighting and struggle. What stamina, what strength of mind and purpose – and all the while, he continued to turn in dazzling, trophy-winning performances for the Reds. By the summer of 1909, as United basked in FA Cup glory, the FA were ready to play their end-game. With the contempt for morality, justice and decency that is the hallmark of every corrupt ruling class – bringing to mind the worst excesses of Thatcherism, indeed – the FA placed a devil's bargain in front of the clubs. If they inserted a clause in every player's contract which barred them from unionisation and forced them to accept, in effect, the primacy of football's law over Parliament's, the FA would declare an amnesty covering every financial and administrative misdemeanour ever perpetrated by the clubs. So much for the FA's "noble fight" to keep the game clean over the past decade – every principle they'd ever espoused was to be jettisoned in order to protect their oily over-privileged hides. The clubs, by majority binding decision, submitted and cast the players to their fate.

Much in the same way that Thatcher's govermnent used prison to persecute poll tax *refuseniks* – a criminal punishment for a civil transgression – the players faced an impossible dilemma. They would lose their livelihoods if they did not sign the new contracts, contracts which demanded they forfeit their legal, political and economic human rights. United players, incredibly, stuck to their beliefs under the leadership of Meredith and Roberts. 1909/10 would begin with the FA Cup winners and Championship favourites banned *sine die* (without a date being given for their return, ostensibly a ban until they agreed to surrender on the League's terms). British football had never seen anything like it. United's players had been catapulted into the vanguard of the Labour movement, cited by the Left as fellow strugglers for justice alongside the miners and shipyard workers. They were truly, now, The Reds.

Sadly, not every player across the nation had the guts of the United lads. As Sandy Turnbull led his boys into United's offices to remove items that they could sell to compensate for their stopped wages, other clubs' players were looking for a way out. The FA saw their chance and played the divide and rule card, offering a new watered-down version of unionisation as a sop to those who signed the new contracts. A nation-wide players' ballot ended 3-1 in favour of taking the deal, which moderates tried to argue would be an incremental step on the way to full rights. It was nothing of the kind, of course: by preventing the players' union from affiliating to the GFTU (the TUC as was), the FA essentially postponed players' emancipation for another half-century. Meredith conceded that, *en masse*, the other clubs' players had not quite lived up to their billing as fighters to rank alongside the miners. But then, no other dressing room had a leadership quite like that of Meredith, Turnbull and Roberts. I daresay the miners' strike would never have been lost if every mine had had a Scargill at the pithead. Leadership matters so much, as United were to discover after Meredith and Turnbull had gone.

On the pitch, as the duo electrified the Clayton crowds, all that off-the-pitch angst was easily forgotten. The day Meredith, Turnbull, Burgess and Bannister came out of the City suspensions to make their United debuts in January 1907 was a public event on a par with Cantona's comeback or

Barcelona '84. Ecstatic Mancunians on the terraces awed watching journos with the delirium of their celebrations for the winning goal – a Meredith-Turnbull one-two, naturally. They couldn't have known that they were witnessing a seismic shift in Mancunian football's tectonic plates but they acted as if they did. With a classic half-back line of Duckworth, Roberts and Bell in place, supporting unbeatable forwards such as the two Turnbulls, Meredith and Wall, United romped to the 1908 championship, the city's first, and collected the club's first FA Cup the season after. Sandy scored the winner in the Final, and top-scored in the title year. If Meredith was the Red king, then Sandy was at least his heir and prince.

Off the field, United's lads were the original roaring boys, regularly out on the town, all living close together, getting up to no good in bookies, breweries and, occasionally, brothels (except for Meredith, who maintained Cantonesque abstemiousness). Just like fans on a night out, the songs would start after the third pint, a mixture of the emerging terrace hits (the Kop DID NOT invent football songs) and bawdy soldier's tunes. Sandy was their Peter Boyle, ever ready to jump atop a table and invent new verses off the top of his head. (The only difference between him and the Boyle is that Sandy was a very good singer and knew what "in the right key" meant.)

Classic English poets often summon up the idyllic images of the two or three years before the mechanised carnage of the Great War descended: the last age of innocence, some have called it. As 1910—11 opened, how beautiful the future must have seemed. We had a new 80,000-capacity luxury stadium, a team playing the cultured, quick-passing game on the deck which became known as the United style for the rest of the century, and a brand new centre forward, Enoch "Knocker" West, whose cannonball shot broke scoring records wherever he went. We stormed to the title, indisputable cocks of the walk in Manchester, Lancashire and the nation.

Yet a visitor to Old Trafford a decade later would have found a grimmer scene. Sandy Turnbull lay dead in an Arras battlefield, and in football disgrace; Meredith was back at City, mourned by thousands of Reds; Knocker West's cannonball would never be seen again, by order of the FA; and United were heading towards Division Two once more, dragging an empty stadium behind them. And it was all the Scousers' fault. (Well, apart from World War One.)

Admittedly, neither Sandy nor Enoch needed much encouragement to get into scrapes and given that both were approaching their twilight years as that last 1914/15 season unfolded, their willingness to cut corners and take risks increased. Sandy was always in and out of bother, whether it was becoming the first player to be sent off in a derby in 1908 (retaliation, as usual) or getting banned by the Club in 1914 for applying much of his foul oath collection to the manager in front of the entire team. Enoch, a Nottingham collier who looked like a sharp-suited 40s spiv, had also been banned for a month in 1911 after a bout of aggro in the middle of a clash with Aston Villa (a cue for yet more provincial paper wars between Mancs and Brummies). And as 1914/15 progressed, team morale was not what it had been; tempers frayed easily, and the spectre of the holocaust on the Western Front naturally made most young men more reckless than usual. Meredith, now over 40, was no longer able to inspire victories on his own and also missed a third of the season through injury. Sandy's dispute with the management, which almost brought all his team-mates out on strike in his support, meant he only played a dozen times. Unthinkably, United were beginning to be threatened by relegation: they found themselves needing to beat Liverpool on Good Friday to keep out of the dreaded drop zone, which tends to have a habit of sucking you down like quicksand once you slip into it late-season.

Liverpool, in comfortable mid-table, were safe – they'd brought quite a few fans with them down the East Lancs. Road but the now infamous rivalry between our clubs was not yet of sufficient power to make this a game they *had* to win. United scored early on through George Anderson and then, well, nothing: as Meredith would later dryly remark in court, "I could see something was wrong." Anderson added a second, eventually, with a facility that looked suspicious, especially against the backdrop of a game played at a semi-trot with barely a decent tackle in 90 minutes. Liverpool, blatantly, were not trying – more curiously, United weren't over-exerting themselves too much either. The players responded to the second goal as if a throw-in had been awarded, almost as if – uh-oh – it had been expected. The Scouse contingent in the crowd, natural experts in matters of chicanery and criminality, twigged what was cooking before anyone else. This was a fix, a rig, a "squared match" as the quaint Edwardian jargon would have it. Eventually, even United fans joined in their catcalls and jeers, despite the fact that the two valuable points had probably pushed United into safety. Match-fixing was what City did, not United – that seemed to be the attitude, as if pulling on the Red jersey should have magically transformed the natures of the ex-Blues within. And indeed it was the ex-Blues Meredith and Turnbull who were the immediate suspects, their City charge-sheets still hanging albatross-like around their necks. But the alleged ring-leader would turn out to be the relative new boy untainted by past City scandal, Enoch West: for once, the guiltiest-looking face did indeed belong to the villain. (Apologies for going on about poor Enoch's untrustworthy features but check out his mugshot in Garth Dykes's outstanding piece of scholarship, *The United Alphabet* – would you have bought a used horse 'n' cart from him?)

That there'd been a fix became embarrassingly obvious. Bookies around the country, who'd taken so many bets on a 2-0 victory that the odds had come down from twelves to 5-1, began refusing to pay out when the eye-witness reports came in. An FA inquiry was inevitable. Doubtless, the FA thought they'd be getting a chance to nail *bête noir* Meredith once and for all. But, remarkably, everyone seemed agreed that for once, the old fox had ducked out. Had he known that this one would be a scam too far? He would emerge from the various hearings unblemished, and played on until his fifties, a living legend unmatched until the reign of Stanley Matthews.

The FA found West and four Liverpool players guilty and banned them all for life. West's case hadn't been helped by evidence from Nottingham bookies that abnormally heavy betting had taken place in his home village of Hucknall Torknard, presumably by friends and relatives in the know. Yet West vehemently protested his innocence and sunk much of his savings into an appeal to the law courts, judging that their brand of justice would be more rigorous than the FA's closed-shop stitch-ups. At first, the case went well for him, with nothing but circumstantial evidence emerging, until Liverpool's Jackie Sheldon took the stand and sang like the proverbial yellow-bellied creature. He testified that West and two other United lads had held a match-rigging summit in the Dog and Partridge (United's prime matchday pub even now) and had organised the whole deal.

Whilst not wishing to defend matchfixing – though the players' grotesque underpayment in those days is surely a mitigating factor – it does appear that the Liverpool players' participation was dramatically more disgraceful than United's. You could argue that there was a certain "noble cause corruption", to use the Met's favourite excuse, in United players wanting to fix a victory: sure, they made some cash, but they also got two vital points to keep United in Division One. Some fans might even argue that anything dodgy is justified for the cause of United. And it's not as though United took bribes to lay down and die like some scummy boxer. But Liverpool did take money to lose and there was no other factor but cash involved. United paid the heaviest price, for the players we lost forever were indubitably superior, and the scandal has always been deemed to reflect more badly on our history rather than on Liverpool's. Still, I guess they received their cosmic payback from the Inter Milan-controlled ref in 1965.

West's case promptly unravelled, and the sneaky George Anderson entered the witness box next day to confirm the scam but claim that he had refused to participate himself. He added that West had made £70 from the wagers (this at a time when the maximum weekly player's wage was £4). The judge, naturally, found against Knocker, who dug up yet more funds (erm, where exactly were these funds coming from, you may well wonder) and went to the Court of Appeal. He lost again, not least because the judges pranged him on his original false claim that he had no relatives in his home village who might, tipped-off, have been responsible for the wagers. Apparently, they found about 60 of them...

Enoch protested his innocence right up until his death in 1965. The playing ban he received was lifted in 1945, but a 59-year-old is hardly likely to get a game from anyone, is he?! (Except, perhaps, from Kenny Dalglish.) George Anderson had got eight months prison in 1918 when it was revealed at another trial that he'd been part of a much larger-scale betting scam well beyond United's parameters. Suddenly, his evidence to the West trial looked even shabbier than it already did. Worst of all, Anderson's testimony had pulled Sandy Turnbull into the frame as a co-conspirator, but his life ban soon became academic when he was blown up by a German shell in 1917 whilst serving with his pals in the footballers' battalion of the Manchester Regiment. In light of what he gave to his country, and of the contribution he made to United on the pitch, few observers allowed his 'disgrace' to be anything more than a minor blemish on his memory. Like the majority of our Red Devils, Sandy's example demonstrates that even the naughtiest bad lads like him and Billy still get to be remembered as legends if they give their all on pitch or in battle.

THE
BRUISER

Later in this book, I'll suggest that Jim Holton was the hardest Red in living memory, and I still think he could've had Roy Keane despite the latter's excellent pugilistic technique. But the hardest of all time? No: that honour must surely go to Frank Barson, who bestrode football after the Great War like a psychotic Colossus. Six feet and thirteen stone of solid Grimethorpe steel, his demonic appetite for ultraviolence dwarfs the reputations of latter-day hardmen such as Vinny Jones or our own King Eric. Sent off at least twelve times in his career, in an era when such punishment tended to be reserved for the perpetrators of straight knock-outs or broken limbs, he simply scared the shit out of strikers throughout the land. Naturally, he played at centre-half, the one position no forward could avoid taking on; and at least until the offside law was changed in 1925, he was the most fearsome in Britain, denied more England caps only because his occasional lawless outbreaks terrified FA selectors. He could play, mind you; there was no-one with greater heading ability in any of England's defences, and he could do ball-tricks with his head that few could manage with their feet. A contemporary cartoonist once drew him as a performing seal, able to do endless keepy-uppies on his 'nose', though most opponents would suggest other more suitable animal similies – like a mad gorilla or charging rhino, for example. As a captain and leader, he was the most inspiring United had until the 50s, a man venerated by his colleagues, the survivors of whom queued to pay tribute to him when he died in 1968. And he had the boyish enthusiasm and sheer drive of a Robson, just the attitude United needed to whip them out of the Second Division into which they'd slumped in 1922.

It was Manchester United's first relegation, and an unmitigated disaster for a club whose finances were becoming extraordinarily perilous. City, still preening in the top flight, had regained the Mancunian top dog status last held when Billy the Wizard was first on their books – and the Scousers had won the Championship. Grim days indeed, and most fans knew where the blame lay: at the heart of the team. United had used six different players at centre-half in 1921/22 to equally dismal effect; without immediate reinforcement, United faced a steamrolling in the notoriously dirty second division. Barson's arrival in August 1922 was thus greeted as a salvation. Everyone in the game knew what Frank Barson could do for a side. Villa had broken the national transfer record for him in 1919 whereupon he'd promptly led them to FA Cup victory. His battling performances had left him with the appearance of a true warrior – a grotesquely mis-shapen nose, the result of one too many breaks, a permanently bruised forehead from a million airborne interceptions, and the iron physique of a middleweight in his prime. If United had to bully their way to the top flight, much as Newton

Heath had done exactly 30 years before, now they had a man to show them how to do it.

It took United three seasons to get back. They just missed out in 1922/3, then farted about in mid-table in 1923/4 when the talismanic Barson suffered two injury lay-offs. But in 1924/5, with Barson at his peak, United finally made it, conceding only 23 goals in their 42 games to set an all-time club defensive record. Frank missed a few games in the spring but came back to lead his lads through an imperious run-in; they kept six clean sheets in the last seven matches. Barson won every Player of the Year Award going and looked set to lay waste to the top flight once more at the venerable age of 34.

Frank would still be playing competitive football well into his forties; given the position he played and the kind of grinding, all-action game he preferred, this made him a physiological marvel of the age. Like Robson decades later, he defied nature itself, for he too liked a pint or ten every now and then (in Frank's case every night). Living next to the Gorse Hill pub in Stretford, he'd roll home at 11.30 with six or seven of his boys after a full evening session, demanding a whopping spread from the kitchen before retiring for a few hours – then he'd be up at 6 for a run and some weight-lifting. He'd always been ox-strong, after working as a blacksmith in his youth and coming through the rigours of wartime, but his indomitability always had the capacity to stun his team-mates. Once, when he'd missed a train to a game, he jogged seven miles through snow drifts and freezing cold to get there on time; on another occasion, he turned up to a rare afternoon training session having already walked from Old Trafford to Northwich and back since daybreak. His method for keeping the beer-belly away was simple and effective: he'd train 'til he dropped, dressed in five or six woolly jumpers, instantly burning off any gramme of fat that dared attach itself to him. He called it "toasting", and contemporaries reported that his routines would have killed lesser men through sheer exhaustion and dehydration. And yet he never seemed to regard his outrageous powers as anything unusual; indeed, many observers put his disciplinary troubles down to the simple fact that he genuinely didn't know his own strength. So he might give a forward what he took to be a gentle cuff for being naughty, but the bloke would helplessly go down like a sack of shit. Referees, unfortunately, tended not to take note of this in mitigation. From fairly early on in his career, you rarely saw his name in print without the prefix "controversial".

Admittedly, there were occasions when he acted knowing his own strength only too well. Frank could sometimes be what we now call "temperamental", generally a euphemism for "psycho". If you wound him up at all in a game – like dare to beat him to the ball – you'd shortly be guaranteed to receive the infamous "Barton Bruiser". This was a kind of shoulder-charge, except that he tended to do it with his head down like a bull, and you counted yourself lucky if it was only upon your shoulder that he impacted. No forward alive was able to stay on his feet when he was targetted for one of these – in fact, few would remain within five yards of their original position. It would be fifty/fifty whether Frank acually played the ball as a result but the point was well made, and only twice did Frank actually get sent off for these bundlings.

Instead, it was his flair for retaliation that tended to account for most of his dismissals. The *Manchester Guardian* once remarked that Frank could be "impetuous", which is an understatement akin to suggesting nuclear fall-out might spoil your rose-beds. Essentially, Frank treated anything out of order as a non-footballing matter and would react to any attempted assaults much as one might outside a pub at 11 o'clock on a Friday night. Retribution would be swift, merciless and often bloody. And yet, more often than not, he'd get away with it. The media scrutiny of today's game would have been terribly alien to the players of the 20s; match reports then were masterpieces of *sang froid*. One second division write-up in 1924, for example, referred to "an incident involving Barson" which resulted in "some words of calm from the referee". What actually happened, according to legend, is that a forward foolhardily attempted to tackle Barson and made the gut-churning error of leaving his foot in. Barson chased him ten yards, clobbered him, and then, when the forward incredibly managed to stay upright, he was rewarded with a Barson 'header'. His piece of personal refereeing completed via that swift dispensation of justice, Frank trotted off back to the game as if nothing had happened – and clearly none the worse for the scything challenge he'd originally received.

There were days, of course, when he couldn't avoid the authorities' attention, such as the 1926 Cup semi-final against City. United were beaten, though happily City lost the final, but most post-match attention was focussed on Barson's treatment of City's own centre-half Sam Cowan. The unsighted ref took no immediate action but could have made his own deductions from the facts. 3.42: Cowan seen bravely entering Barson's personal space. 3.42 and three seconds: Cowan sparked out unconscious on the deck as Barson drops to his haunches, unconvincingly feigning accidental collision. In a packed Bramhall Lane, with 25,000 howling Bluenoses and an entire press corps as witnesses, Barson was not going to escape as lightly as usual. The FA later banned him for two months. For the rest of the match, Barson had to hold his fire as the ref never took his eyes off him. With City already a disgracefully illegal goal up, and Barson effectively neutered, City romped to a 3-0 victory, making an infamous brace with the 6-1 panning they'd given a Barton-less United at Old Trafford three months earlier. Barton, unusually for a United hero, never created any derby legends for himself – in fact, he never played in a side that beat City. During the aeon between the Russian Civil War and the German invasion of Poland, United only beat City twice. Hard to believe, kids, but for two decades we were the Bitters of inter-war Manchester.

That afternoon marked the moment when Frank began to roll gently down the other side of the hill. The new offside law had left him and his breed if not obsolete, then certainly obsolescent. Moreover, he was heading into his late 30s, facing nippy little sods barely out of school – he'd only play 30 more games for United. When the Reds finally, reluctantly, released him to Watford in 1928, they knew they were losing just about the only true jewel in United's base metal crown. The immediate post-Barton era would be a gloomy and desperate one, as United headed seemingly inexorably for both bankruptcy and Division Three. The heady days of early 1926, when Barton was driving United towards Wembley and a top three league berth, would suddenly seem like as ancient a history as the Meredith glory days.

Barson still raged against the dying light. One extraordinary afternoon in October 1926 provided testimony of his almost inhuman resilience. Playing against his old mates of Aston Villa, a Barson Bruiser had gone spectacularly wrong, leaving Frank with a couple of broken bones and open bleeding wounds. Off he went, obviously not to return, and in this pre-substitute era United faced tough opponents with ten men. Unbelievably, within minutes, who should trot out of the Old Trafford tunnel, a little unsteady and heavily strapped up, but Frank. He'd apparently told the trainer, "I'm not leaving my boys alone out there" and insisted he played on through the pain. United stuck him out on the wing, much as we would one day do with Ray Wood in a Cup Final, just for nuisance value. Instead, Barson continued to barge his way into the game and sensationally scored the key goal in the 2-1 victory. Later, it would be discovered that he'd been so badly hurt that even this behemoth would be unable to train or play for the next fortnight. The perhaps apocryphal pay-off has it that he also refused painkillers, claiming that several pints would do the trick just as well. Hard? There were softer diamonds than Frank. This, after all, was a player whose bonce was such a rock that he once scored with a header in driving rain from thirty-three yards. If you've ever felt a pre-war football when it's wet, you'll understand why even writing that line makes me feel queasy.

To his detractors, the 20s equivalents of your Linekers and Charltons, Barson was dirty and violent – a terrorist in baggy shorts. Think about how you feel towards Souness or McMahon and you'll be able to empathise. But there's another difference between Barson and the modern assassins (apart, that is, from being a Red, and therefore to us a *freedom-fighter* in baggy shorts.) You all know who I'm thinking about when I suggest that most of the 80s and 90s hardmen also bore reputations for being shits off the field too, legendarily arrogant, amoral and mercenary. Barson, by contrast, was universally loved by those fortunate enough to be in the trenches on his side of the wire. It wasn't just that they admired his powers – the legendary Club official Louis Rocca, for example, saying of him that "in all my life, I never saw a man who could get more out of his team than Frank Barson." It was that he had a gruff modesty and a genuine care for others, especially younger team-mates. At Villa, he'd voluntarily looked after their celebrated youth team, the Villa Colts, and he continued that concern at United. When he was released in 1928, there was a young lad called Tommy Barnett who'd been let go because he wasn't going to make the Division One grade. As the pair stood outside the manager's office on dismissal day, Tommy had tears in his eyes as he muttered, "What's to become of me?" Frank turned to him and said, "You stick with me son, I'll see you're all right." And he did: Frank first insisted that Watford had to take young Tommy as well as himself, and then got him deals at other clubs to ensure he had a career.

Not that anyone would have dared praise him to his face for his philanthropy, for he was almost allergic to flattery and congratulation. When United bought him a pub as a thank-you present for almost single-handedly wrenching them back into Division One, Frank went down to the Ardwick Green hostelry to take the keys. Inside, fans were holding a riotous party in his honour and Reds from miles around were said to be on their way to pay homage. After fifteen minutes, he was so overwhelmed by the discomfort and embarrassment this acclamation was causing him that he chucked the keys to a server and told him the pub was his from now on. Then he scuttled back to the Gorse for a quiet session with his mates. He'd done his job, that was all: no need for all this 'hero' nonsense.

Ten years after he left, a fan wrote in a memoir of being at the front of the terraces when Frank was coming in to tackle a player from behind by the touchline. "In all the noise and excitement, you still heard him coming from the distance, as though the very ground quaked under his boots. That poor soul in front of us must have felt that the horsemen of the apocalypse themselves were upon him. What a sight and sound that was!" Truly this Red Devil was the finest Hell had to offer.

THE
BOGOTÁ
BANDIT

If there was one era in Old Trafford's history when the kind of
Red Devilry we've been talking about seemed thin on the
ground, then it was the decade or so after the Second World
War. From Matt Busby's appointment as manager until the
Munich disaster, United acquired a reputation for clean-living
decency and moral probity quite out of kilter with the Club's
previous – and subsequent – history. And, barring the odd
blemish such as irregular payments to youth teamers' families
in the mid-50s and bouts of Cup Final ticket-touting, the
saintly reputation was well-founded. Much of this was, of
course, due to Matt Busby himself, whose aura of inner
strength and incorruptibility impressed all observers from the
outset. As journalists and colleagues grew to know him, it
became utterly inconceivable to them that anything but the
highest standards could be operating at United – not under
the aegis of such a magisterial character. The press rarely bothered to keep their ears open for Old Trafford naughtiness,
because it was so evidently a waste of journalistic time. Long

before Munich, United were coming to be seen as an exemplary institution, one that could be universally respected, emulated, even loved: world-wide supporters' clubs began sprouting up years before 1958 and contrary to popular myth, United were already many English fans' second-favourite club by the mid-50s. Munich transformed that development into an epidemic, admittedly, but the roots of United's world-club status lay in what Matt made United represent from 1945 onwards, not in the wreckage of that plane.

The rogues' gallery of Barson, Turnbull, Meredith and Hell's Heathens now seemed to belong to a different universe. The 1930s, United's worst playing decade, had perversely helped lay the ground for this new, almost holy, United. Virtually free of all scandal, United in the Thirties were known for just two things: financial disaster and desperate footballing decline. When a club is saved from bankruptcy at the 11th hour, or only escapes relegation to the Third Division on the last day of a season, or appears to visitors like a ghost town as its 70,000 capacity stadium remains 90 per cent empty, the general popular response is not loathing or fear but pity. Youngsters will recognise it as the City Syndrome. Everyone loves those plucky, gallows-humoured Bluenoses as they reel from one catastrophe to another, still turning up *en masse* every week for more of the same. United in the 30s were beneficiaries of the same pathetic sympathy. Their only scandal, the Neil Dewar affair of 1934, was thus typical of the new atmosphere, being comedic rather than outrageous. United were no longer match-fixers, hardmen and rebels – they were lovestruck players who'd elope with directors' daughters, as Dewar did to much tabloid amusement. There was an impression that once United had been punished for their past transgressions by enduring a decade of suffering, they could start the post-war era with a clean slate.

Having our ground blitzed by Uwe Rosler's ancestors only added to the credit column: now we were brave homeless Mancs, dossing down at our greedy neighbour's ground, somehow contriving to build a brilliant team nonetheless. The kind of players we had in 1946 had opponents purring too – no nasty psychos or arrogant bastards, just a decent bunch of mainly local good-sports, many of whom had served their country in the war or, in the youngsters' cases, had come up through United's admirable MUJAC scheme (Man Utd Junior Athletics Club). Who could hate a team of self-effacing war heroes and youth team graduates? Especially when, as became rapidly obvious, they were playing the style of beautiful, fast-paced, attacking football the bumper crowds were happy to pay two bob to witness.

Charlie Mitten was one of the most beautiful and pacey players of them all. Claiming the outside-left spot for the duration of his United career, he'd lost six of his best winging years to the War but at the age of 24 was determined to make up for lost opportunities. There are plenty of old Reds who'll tell you that the forward line he played in was the most perfectly integrated and exciting offensive quintet ever seen at Old Trafford: Delaney, Morris, Rowley, Pearson and Mitten tripped off the tongue of every football connoisseur. That line-up took United to three consecutive runners-up spots in the Championship and, most gloriously, to victory in the 1948 Cup Final, widely acknowledged to be the best ever played. The whole run had been the kind of rip-roaring adventure from which United's legend is woven – drawn away every round against good opposition, they cracked on to the Final without a replay, scoring eighteen goals along the way and another four in the Final. Charlie, who was consistent and reliable as well as brilliant, played in every match and contributed mightily to nullifying Stan Matthews at Wembley; later, he'd play 113 consecutive matches for United, rattling in goals too with a regularity no other winger could match. He was a crowd favourite, a Busby favourite and a team-mates' favourite – the Fifties lay ahead, ready for him to claim as his own. Instead, he would become a bandit, an outcast, a forgotten man – as the papers later billed him, "Cheeky Charlie – Soccer Outlaw".

Cheeky he certainly was, Old Trafford's prime rogue along-side fellow piss-takers and occasional goat-actors, Johnny Aston and Henry Cockburn. Not that he was the riotous, 80s-style self-abusing type – like Meredith before him, he never smoked or drank and maintained a rigorous personal regimen – just that he would be the one to lift the spirits on a cold, post-defeat morning with a well-timed one-liner or shaggy dog story. Or come up with a catch-phrase with which to taunt a team-mate. Or simply provide the day's best grey-hound tip for the lads (and the manager) to look forward to that afternoon. It's the sort of role David May seems to like to think he has today (with the exception that everyone admired and loved Charlie). And Charlie was cool, in the smart-kid-at-the-back-of-the-class kind of way; he played like he lived, producing excellence with what appeared to be the minimum of effort, to the consternation of the drones at teacher's knee who have to sweat blood for every advance.

Charlie had that golden touch about him, as if he were one of life's chosen ones, the type who always emerges from scrapes unscathed. He'd had it in the war, when his training crew somehow escaped disciplinary sanctions after accidental-ly shooting down one of our own aircraft, or when a chance meeting with Stanley Matthews got him off the fast-track to dangerous airplane gunnery and into a cushy PE instruction job. This was just the touch an inveterate gambler needed; you never saw Charlie at the ground before 2.30 on a match-day as he'd still be at the bookie's, almost certainly collecting his winnings. Matt Busby liked Charlie in any event, but their shared passion for the track provided an extra bond. Sometimes their relationship resembled that of Milo and the Colonel in *Catch-22*, as Matt eagerly tagged along with Charlie's latest wheeze. The night Charlie pretended to invent a Magic Potion for a greyhound from a concoction of the various embrocations available at Old Trafford was typical. Jimmy Murphy and Matt were gagging to get to the track, cramming into a car with Charlie and his mates, apparently ready to blow half a week's money on the magic mutt. Charlie never let on that his Magic Potion was a crock – and the dog won anyway. That was lucky Charlie all over. But in 1950, his luck ran out, and what was once thought of as his big break instead broke the back of his career.

In many ways, the lot of the professional footballer had changed little since Billy Meredith's day. In essence, they all remained underpaid wage-slaves, tied like serfs to the retain-and-transfer system, unable legally to earn more than £14 a week. Most United players lived in extremely modest club-owned semis, for which a deduction was made from their wage packet, and drove second-hand bangers: it was simply unheard of for a player, however grand, to go out and buy some flash roadster as they do today. £14 a week – assuming a player ever rose to that maximum, for one effect of a cap was to deflate wages all-round – was a standing incentive for that old club stand-by, the brown envelope, to come into effect. But even that was denied at United. Matt bluntly refused to countenance it: whatever his views on the desirability or otherwise of the maximum wage, rules were rules and no man of honour could accept transgressions. He was not yet strong enough a power at Old Trafford to go shouting the odds to the Board either, and it was tricky enough a battle for him to secure even a proper allocation of Cup Final tickets for the players, who were also on a much smaller bonus to win than their opponents or past winners.

Yet any player could look around and see the wealth cascading into the game. All sports flourished massively after the war as a relieved nation flocked towards an exploding leisure industry. You even got 50,000 at Belle Vue's speedway matches, for God's sake – if it moved, sung or flickered on a screen, thousands would queue up to pay to see it. United regularly drew over 70,000 to watch them at Maine Road and broke most records away from 'home' too, as Charlie's boys became the biggest travelling draws in the game. Many leading clubs were posting profits which would today be equivalent to £10 million, and that's just what they declared on-book. Meanwhile, players, many of whom were trying to compensate for six lost earning years, were being told that nothing could change as far as they were concerned. There was an attitude amongst the ruling class, evident in many spheres of national activity, that the plebs should feel lucky to be alive and be grateful for what they were getting. Industrial production soared, yet inflation and wage rises remained negligible; the Empire's food markets were all restored, yet rationing remained in place until 1951's "bonfire of controls". When the team went on a U.S. tour in 1950, and saw for the first time in their lives how a real consumerist society operates, many were stunned. They finally realised how poor they really were, given the scarce and highly marketable skills they possessed, and how abundant the pleasures were outside Britain's umbrella of austerity.

At that sensitive juncture, as Charlie reflected on his paltry material circumstances after enjoying his best season yet (ever-present, 16 goals), Bogotá came calling. FC Santa Fe in Colombia wanted to sign Charlie and were offering him the equivalent of a lifetime's UK earnings in just his first season. It was brilliant timing, catching him in the glamorous environs of New York, possibly when the balance of his mind was disturbed by the temptation all around. After all, the team had been mixing with big-shots and movie-stars, seeing how the Other Half lived and realising, dumbfoundedly, that they by right should belong to that Other Half. How could Mitten go back to half-pints in dingy Stretford public bars when champagne in plush Bogota villas was on offer?

The money was too good to refuse, the lifestyle too exotically irresistible – to a self-confident adventurous spirit like Charlie's, there could only be one answer. He told Matt he was going to accept in the manager's New York hotel room; Matt, flabbergasted, told him he couldn't go. But Charlie's contract had expired and he could refuse to re-sign. Normally, United would then be able to prevent him from playing anywhere in the world unless he re-signed, or unless they decided to sell him. But Colombia wasn't a member of FIFA and could consequently tell all the world's blazered bigwigs exactly where to go. Only money talked in Colombia, and Mitten needed no translation.

Amusingly, Charlie claims that he told Matt exactly how much he was going to earn, and that Matt replied wryly, "Do they need a manager?" Actually, Matt had just signed a massive new deal with United worth £60 a week basic, weeks after Spurs had tried to tempt him away with a similarly hefty offer. A few years later, Real Madrid would offer "heaven and earth" to persuade Matt to abandon United for the Bernabeu, but Matt refused, saying that Old Trafford was already heaven on earth. Matt never seemed to tell Charlie this, but to him there were things more important than money and that experience would teach you that truth. Mitten, only in his twenties, would need to discover that for himself.

They would part 'correctly', like gentlemen, but not warmly. Matt was devastated to lose a player he always admitted was "irreplaceable"; he also felt personally hurt that Mitten would leave the family he'd built at OT just for grubby cash; and he was outraged by the possibility of other players being 'infected' by the Colombian virus, as fellow japesters Cockburn and Aston were also tapped up for transfer. (Managers have problems with Colombian influences in the dressing room these days, of course, though of a rather different nature...) If Charlie was full of breezy promises about possible returns to England and Manchester, Matt was not so forthcoming. Busby and Ferguson have this in common: you could not cross them and expect not to pay for it.

Whilst the footballing establishment howled in anger at Mitten's 'treachery', one old pro came down to Piccadilly to see the young rebel off – Billy Meredith. Suddenly, Old Trafford was reconnected to its old tradition: in the midst of this saintly era, a flash of the old Red Devilry sparked, as rebels a generation apart said their farewells. Billy was there as the Players' Union rep, and left Charlie in no doubt that he would have made exactly the same choice himself. He kept to himself the further observation that should Charlie ever decide to return, a 1909-style execution would surely await.

Mitten enjoyed the high life in Colombia to the max, playing alongside Alfredo di Stefano, mixing with tycoons and stars, waited on by servants and maids and, of course, coining it in big-style. He even fulfilled a lifetime goal by becoming a racehorse owner, in an era when the idea of a footballer owning anything other than a pair of old boots and a few medals was deemed suspiciously ambitious. But, as with so many footballing adventurers to come, the familial responsibilities he'd taken on were to sink his rebellion. The wife was homesick, and the boy needed 'proper' English schooling. Reluctantly, in a manner Paul Ince might recognise, the Red rebel would have to come home. Matt, like Fergie, would not exactly be waiting with open arms.

The press treated his return as one can imagine they would do with Ronnie Biggs. The Soccer Outlaw was back to face his *High Noon* with United and the authorities – a metaphorical blood-bath seemed inevitable. For Mitten had not just taken the money and run – he'd revelled in a barrage of press coverage, lambasting the outmoded FA and warning the English game that if it didn't adapt to the new methods he'd witnessed out there, England would be humiliated on the world stage. 1953's Magyars would prove his point, of course. No administrator would be interested in what Charlie had to say, save for "Guilty as charged". The FA hauled him in front of a tribunal, banned him for six months and fined him another six months' wages on top. United refused to enter any pleas on his behalf, told him he would be transferred as soon as possible, and added their own hefty fine. He wouldn't be allowed to train at the ground either – as far as they were concerned, he was no longer a Red. Personal pleas to Matt went largely unheeded: he'd announced his Faustian pact in that New York hotel room and now he had to pay the price. Fans split over the issue: to some, he'd betrayed the Club and had to go; to others, he had justice on his side and he was too good a player to discard. He played on for Fulham and Mansfield before becoming manager at Newcastle – a brutal assessment would be that he might not have got into the United team for more than a season after his 1951 return anyway. From Matt's point of view, when issues of loyalty, the law and personal propriety were at stake, acceding to Charlie's pleas for a second chance would have been a poor bargain. It had been a tough human sacrifice at the altar of abstract principle but as Matt had shown with Johnny Morris, and would show again with Johnny Giles, it was an exchange he was always prepared to make.

So once again a rebellious United spirit had brought the plight of his fellow workers to national attention, and once again the brotherhood of players had been defeated. But for the rest of the decade, the issue never left the top of football's agenda. Season after season, as more and more brown envelope irregularities were uncovered and players singled out for exemplary punishment, the racket presided over for seventy years by the FA continued to stink up the game. Ironically, Charlie would find himself at the centre of the struggle's end-game in 1961, when the Eastham case finally broke the FA's stranglehold and released the serfs from their masters' bondage. Rather embarrassingly, Mitten was technically by that point one of masters, a defendant party to the case in his capacity as manager of Newcastle at the time the affair ignited. His conduct during the months dominated by headlines about the case was not wholly well-regarded; some have suggested that his supposed sympathy should have translated more evidently into useful purpose on Eastham's behalf. He himself left questions dangling when he told his biographer that "now I was on the management side, I could see both arguments." Eastham's victory should have covered Mitten in glory, for it was the final vindication of the priciples for which he and Meredith had fought, but the compromised position he had to take denied him full reward. Perhaps, at last, he'd finally had a taste of what it must have been like to be Matt Busby in 1950, struggling to stay honourable, successful and sympathetic simultaneously, an almost impossible task in football. One wonders if then, in hindsight, Charlie might have wished he'd stepped back to see the bigger picture in 1950 and declined the Colombian carrot? When Matt denied Real to stay at "heavenly" Old Trafford, perhaps he demonstated that he'd learned a lesson that came just a touch too late for Mitten.

Charlie's still alive, a sprightly 77, watching the progress of various relatives involved in the game. The footballers haven't made it yet and the one who's shown most of Charlie's ambition and cheekiness is great-nephew and journalist Andy, who somehow manages to straddle the spiritually mutually antagonistic horses of *United We Stand* and the *Man Utd Magazine*. Fortunately – and unusually amongst budding hacks – Uncle Charlie's yen for Bogotá has not inspired in him any interest in modern Colombian produce whatsoever. He's also disappointed not to possess Uncle's ball skills. But, these days, who does?

THE
LEEDS
LUCIFER

I'm fairly sure that somewhere in the Bible, there's a story about how Lucifer came into existence. Apparently, he was once God's right-hand man, his number one angel and main bro', but there was some kind of aggro that resulted in him falling from grace and taking up residence in the basement, whereupon he became evil incarnate as the Fallen One, Beelzebub, Old Nick and so on. George Lucas used the same idea in his *Star Wars* trilogy, which is stuffed with Christian symbolism, whereby Darth Vader turns out to have once been a goodie who was tempted over to the Dark Side by some Norman Tebbit clone. Following this analogy, Johnny Giles, then, is United's Darth Vader: the heir apparent to all that was good and Busbyite, turned by the malevolent Don Revie into the personification of football in the 1965—75 Dark Ages.

Few Reds, whether they're youngsters who only know him from his *Express* outpourings or oldies who grimly recall bloody Wars of the Roses past, have a good word for him. But some, who saw him during his four United first-team years, still wonder what might have been if the Fallen One hadn't got away. If he and Busby had avoided their 1963 disagreement, what kind of influence could he have brought to bear on United? Instead of becoming a purveyor of cynical Revieism, might he not have had a key hand in modernising Busbyism to take us beyond 1968 to further success, rather than decline and relegation? Just as a player, imagine what he could have added: a midfield featuring the game's three greatest passers of the ball – Giles, Charlton and Crerand – would surely have been completely unbeatable. Sure, we didn't do too badly without him, did we? But as Matt himself admitted as early as 1964, selling Giles had been his worst ever mistake. And what pleasure Giles took in returning to haunt us, denying us two Cup Finals and tormenting us during our post-Busby demise. Even now, he continues to tackle us from behind, harrying United in his column, taking a lead in the 'Hang Cantona' movement of '95, surely often causing Fergie to choke on his kedgeree as he reads his favourite morning paper. Hard to believe that this "Man The Players Read" used to be accused of being gutless at United for both timid play and his refusal to take sides in dressing room debates. Nowadays, the first characteristics that spring to Red minds are his unwanted tabloid opinions and his part in Leeds' brutal tactics. And, admittedly, the divine ball-playing skill of a one-time Busby Babe.

What a pedigree this man had. Signed from Home Farm in the summer of 1956, he thus arrived at Old Trafford during the most mystical, magical era in our history: anyone on the United staff at that time has always gone through life surrounded by the aura of having played with immortals. Moreover, he was part of the now legendary Behan chain, the succession of brilliant Irish lads discovered and shipped over to Manchester by Billy Behan. (Billy's boys included Johnny Carey, Lian Whelan, Tony Dunne and Paul McGrath.) Furthermore, Matt saw him as special, a player with the kind of intelligence and pure ball skill he'd always venerated. Giles had everything going for him – here was an assured Manchester United star of the future, and most observers knew it.

Yet in the early 60s, United's dressing room and training ground were not happy places; in such a festering atmosphere even one so apparently fated to succeed faced internal criticism and doubters. United were suffering a sort of delayed post-Munich malaise, when for a few years the Club seemed unsure of its direction, which led some to doubt Matt's capacity to restructure. The dream of a youth-built team had died with the players at Munich; now Matt had to compromise his ideals and shell out for a few acquisitions. But the mix of personalities never gelled either on or off the field, and there were plenty of potential rogues and Red Devils besides Giles. Loud, forceful, dominant men such as Harry Gregg were joined by later imports Noel Cantwell, Maurice Setters and court jester Albert Quixhall: the combined fee total for this quartet was over £130,000, a huge amount for the early 60s. Arguably, none of these purchases was as successful as Matt had hoped they'd be and, as an aggregation, they perhaps shook things up off-field more than was desirable. Throughout the 1960—63 period, the politicking and debating led in particular by Cantwell and Setters, which often centred on the Busby managerial methodology, sapped the spirit but contributed little to our displays – flirting with relegation as we did between '62 and '63 seemed to testify to that. The team was less than the some of its parts; perfect for one-off Cup displays, which saw us reach two Cup semi-finals, going on to win the trophy in '63, but useless in the grinding league.

There was darker, black-tinged Red Devilry afoot too, if the rumours were to be believed: match-fixing. Urban legends about dodgy games are a staple of football, more so in the days of the maximum wage restrictions which virtually incited players to cheat. Nor was it historically unknown at United, as the 1915 case had demonstrated. The explosion of scandal, when it finally showered Tony Kay and Co. in 1963, thankfully affected Sheffield Wednesday but it could so easily have been United. The *Daily Mail* progressed as far in their investigations as to send reporters up to United's hotel in Blackpool to front up Harry Gregg and certain others with allegations of conspiracy to fix matches during the period 1960—62. Harry was in the frame simply because he was the keeper, the 'bookies' friend' position, but he was actually the most outraged United player on this issue, the only one to go on the record over the years and claim that he refused several times to participate in fixes. Gregg has told journalists that United matches were rigged and has even named players whom he alleges were involved. One or two he alleges are big names, and one is still a major player in the football commercial world whose exposure now could ruin him. Gregg, as I write, is penning his autobiography: it remains to be seen whether any publisher's libel lawyer would allow him to print the names and match details. I doubt it – and certainly the *Daily Mail* never gathered enough conclusive evidence to go to press, although they were at least on the brink of specifying three of the allegedly dodgy matches concerned. Matt was, of course, utterly scandalised by the mere thought that any of his players could have been involved and promised to show the door to anyone even suspected of the crime. The 60s were turning out to be a harsh, dour decade (or so it seemed before the glorious outburst of 1963/4 when United were transformed into Champions-in-waiting) and the innocent days of the original Busby Babes must have seemed long gone.

Albert Quixhall would probably have been the last to get involved in such shenanigans, although he was the one player whose sometimes inexplicably appalling displays would have unfairly had terrace wags waving brown paper bags at him, had they known about the allegations. A record £45,000 buy, dubbed the "Golden Boy" first by admiring pressmen, then later by sarcastic team-mates, his goal every three games was simply not enough. A strange, nervous performer who careered from blinders to disasters like an early Andy Cole, he became the team joker whose speciality was crapping into players' shoes. That, and his unique ball-trick which bewitched youngsters as much as Cruyff's did a decade later and caused just as many sprained ankles, tend to be all he's remembered for today. Behind his back, the team loudmouths also accused him of being a "cheat", too ready to dive or hide when the going got tough. The likes of Maurice Setters, a hard-faced hard-edged sergeant-major, hated puffy play: and even Giles was thought to be too weak-kneed for the fight, an opinion apparently shared by Busby and Jimmy Murphy too but not one that would survive in the game much longer once he'd gone to Leeds.

Giles' position in all the politics was curious. He wasn't one of the seniors shouting the odds, even though he shared many of their opinions about the need for Busby to get modernising, nor did he quite belong to the other '56 boys, who kept their heads down and opinions to themselves but generally resented anything that could be construed as anti-Busbyite. Giles, already, was getting a reputation for being very smart, self-possessed, arrogant even, someone who'd do his own fighting for himself when the time came. One or two resented him for it, wondering why he didn't support the demands for new methods; at a famous clear-the-air meeting in 1962, for example, Giles dismissed the entire exercise as a "waste of time", infuriating some of his fellow players.

What did get Giles going was the more selfish concern of where he was playing in the team. He wanted to be inside-right but Busby kept putting him out on the wing. Hindsight says Giles was right, for he became a great at Leeds at inside-right and then as a proper midfielder, but at the time Busby felt he knew what he was doing. After all, Giles had been given a chance there in '61/2 and had blown it, playing particularly poorly in the Cup semi-final defeat. Giles blamed a viral infection for his failure and wasn't prepared to wait much longer. The example of Bobby Charlton, who played brilliantly on the wing for many years before finally getting the central berth he wanted, was used by management as an example: play for the team, wait your turn and all will come good. But the final parting of the ways between Busby and Giles was never really about a clash of opposites taking its toll. In fact, it was the similarity of the men at that stage which created the problem, an unusual and intriguing conjunction that many found incomprehensibly enigmatic.

Neither man really cared about money: the greatest debates for them concerned the game itself, and how it should be played. Busby had no problem handling the never-ending procession of players whingeing about bonuses but facing an intelligent advocate whose sole motivation was playing and winning posed different problems. Both had strong opinions and beliefs but were happier not to be shouting the odds about them, thus running the risk that they might be misunderstood by less subtle minds; both were masters of the one-on-one mind-games that take place in serious debate. And both, crucially, were intensely proud men who sought secure self-possession. Giles had one Busby tactic sussed – the ploy of dropping someone by asking them how they were playing, then using the response as leverage to get them to accept a rest. It usually went thus: "How do you think you played last week, son?" The player, trying to be both modest and careful, replies, "OK" or "Not bad" or "I'm always trying to improve." Whereupon Matt would pounce and make his next sentence conclude, "...and let's see if a rest brings you back a better player." Game over. But when, after the '63 semi, Busby pulled this on Giles, the canny Irishman was ready. "How do you think you did, son?" asked Matt. "Well!" replied Johnny confidently, before startling Matt by immediately adding stridently: "That's what I think – what do you reckon?" "Er, yes, you played reasonably well," muttered Matt. "So why are you planning to leave me out then?" inquired Giles, getting his retaliation in first, "for if I played 'reasonably well' and we won a Cup semi-final but you're still about to tell me I'm dropped then I've got no chance, have I?" Giles had signalled that he wasn't prepared to kowtow anymore, that he wouldn't go along with the rotation and resting tactics Matt liked to deploy. Here was a still-raw 22-year-old, essentially telling Britain's greatest manager that he couldn't call the shots any-more. Matt reacted like you would expect Alex Ferguson to in a similar situation – he accepted the first safe offer for Giles that came along.

At least, he thought it was safe. In 1963, Leeds United were a struggling Second Division outfit, as far away from United's universe as Inter Milan were when Fergie offloaded Ince. But just as Ince may well one day succeed in wreaking vengeance via the unforeseen plot-twist of Liverpool buying him, Giles was promptly afforded a similar opportunity courtesy of Leeds's remarkable transformation. Within 18 months, Giles would be spearheading a Tyke challenge that threatened two of United's 1965 trophy ambitions. Whereas Matt expressed regret that they'd fallen out over so apparently trivial an issue, Giles never did so. The evil Empire turned him too successfully.

Leeds United were the football anti-heroes of the twelve years following Giles's transfer. Symbolically, their reign of terror exactly coincided with the duration of Giles's stay there, as though Lucifer's presence brought them strength. A month after reaching their zenith, the 1975 European Cup Final, Giles left Elland Road, and Leeds's empire crumbled as spectacularly as the Dark Star exploded. Giles loved the Leeds regime and shamelessly reminisces about it. He explicitly makes the comparison with shambolic (*sic*) Busby United, crooning over the Revie dossiers, the obsessive attention to defensive tactics, the heavy drill of organisation and rotating gamesmanship. The latter, a Leeds invention, particularly typified the club – that players should take it in turn to commit bad fouls in order to spread the risk around, rather than have one hothead do everything and then get sent off. That any club should even be actively thinking on these lines said everything about where the glory game was heading. One Giles quote summed up the overall style-less living death they called successful football: "Basically we would cut down the goals against and win games scoring fewer goals." Leeds were perfecting series of dreary 1-0 wins long before these were a twinkle in Arsenal's eye. Uniquely, they won the 1969 title scoring less goals than they gained points. Football, Leeds-style, was no longer a branch of showbiz, but a version of trench warfare. As Paddy Crerand said in the late 60s as he watched the stampede abandoning Busbyite traditions to embrace Leeds's new world order: "If, one day, all the tacticians reached perfection, the result would be a 0-0 draw – and there would be nobody there to see it."

Johhny Giles, along with Norman Hunter and Billy Bremner, is forever associated in the public's mind with that era and mentality. Giles was especially emblematic of Leeds, for on his day he was as magical a player as any, just as the '73/4 Leeds side could enthrall along with the best of the entertainers. But just as often he was the epitome of Leeds' reductive and brutal style. And it is right that their legacy in the popular memory reflects this. Denis Law, who tends to understatement, still summarised Leeds thus:

"They brought a new 'professional' attitude of 'win at all costs'. Their tactics resembled a commando raid: knock out the main installations – the key ball-players – then get on with the job. Gamesmanship and the professional foul became their hallmark. They played some magnificent football in their later years but people in the game never forgave them for their original tactics."

And as for Giles personally, George Best for example still spittingly recalls one typical incident:

"At the start of a match, Giles said to me, 'Why can't you be a gentleman, like Bobby Charlton?' An hour into the game, he came in over the top...he brings his boot down on the shinbone, splits the guard and cuts my leg open. Then he said to me again, 'Why can't you be a gentleman like Bobby Charlton?'"

A mad movie-villain quality to that, don't you think? Joe Pesci in *Goodfellas* springs to mind.

Giles now lectures footballers in his column and elsewhere in the media, sometimes bizarrely taking the moral high ground as he did with Eric Cantona. A colleague of mine who's well-acquainted with several footballers from the Giles era remarks, with some understatement, that the Leeds brutality is not remembered fondly. Those players, who were kicked from pillar to post by Giles and his chums during the filthy clashes of that decade, still believe in the old pre-Revie values: that you don't seek to "win at all costs", that you should at least try to be sporting and decent, that football is about glory not merely success. Maybe one day Giles will take off that hard mask, Darth Vader style, and reveal the old Red below, maybe to admit that in his heart of hearts he wished that fateful 1963 showdown had never occurred, that he might be remembered today by the general public as lovingly as are Law, Best and Charlton. Giles is admired, no doubt, and respected for his achievements and talent, but it's the cold admiration of a bitter war foe, much as that of a Tommy for the Wehrmacht. Giles fought well, but the Leeds cause was ignoble and destructive of all that is good about football. That trip he took in the summer of '63 was further than the 30 miles from Manchester to Leeds – it was from footballing heaven to hell.

THE
BEST

Who could possibly claim to outrank George Best for Red Devilry? It was always, in hindsight, particularly appropriate that he got dubbed the Fifth Beatle in 1966, for he claims an equivalent position in football culture as the Fabs do in pop's. For the extraordinary truth about The Beatles was that they were not only complete originals, pioneers who opened creative paths for others to follow, but that it turns out they were also unsurpassable. They went further, and more successfully, down every track than anybody else has managed since. That surprised the rock crit. establishment but it's now accepted: no-one can ever emulate the impact of *Sgt. Pepper*, no guitar sound will ever out-thrill John and George's on *Revolver*, no melodicist will ever match McCartney's 1965—69 virtuosity. So too George Best; he showed what was possible in every sphere, and then sat back to watch hundreds fail in attempts to outdo him.

Those wiseacres who used to claim that Best would historically be seen to have somehow 'failed' by quitting OT at 27 have been proved hopelessly wrong. The legend burns brighter than ever – he's still winning Greatest Sportsman Of All Time awards even now, despite the myriad embarrassments of his last 20 years. Three decades before Cantona repopularised the concept, he was the first footballer to take advantage of the mass media age and demonstrate conclusively to the watching world that football could be an art as well as a sport. That a footballer could be as showbiz as Sinatra, and have as great a cultural impact outside his immediate profession. And that a working class Modern Lad could squeeze more hedonistic pleasure out of life than ever previously imagined. The Roaring Twenties and the Naughty (Eighteen) Nineties might have witnessed much infamous decadence, but it had been a lifestyle reserved for the upper crust's *jeunesse dorée*. Best and the other 60s proletarian icons – Lennon, Caine, Burton *et al*. – killed working class deference and humility forever. Today's urban and sometimes urbane casual boys, with their attitude, style and live-life-to-the-max philosophies, are all sons of Best in a way.

He is, of course, also the most written-about player of all time, Best literature dwarfing even the voluminous output dedicated to Pelé, Cantona and Maradona. Every sports scribe since the 60s has felt it necessary to have a go, from the studious portentousness of McIllvaney via the knowing insight of Parkinson right down to the trashy, ghost-written, dreck levels more familiar in the 90s. A remarkably varied and exciting life, experienced by a fascinating and complex personality, is hardly encapsulable in one chapter herein – few footballers, indeed, have merited multiple biographies as much as George has. That must be some source of pleasure to him, for biographies of brilliant people were always his favourite reading matter, and he's acutely aware of, and sensitive to, his own historical legacy. I would recommend the book he co-wrote with Michael Parkinson for an unbeatable mixture of pathos, bathos and downright naughtiness, if you can find it. Meanwhile, here's some Scenes From A Life where George is at his best, or worst, depending on your morality.

1964

There's two ways for an alcoholic to get started. The Barney Gumble version has a previously clean-living abstemious chap thrust accidentally towards a can of blob, who swigs it down and bellows, "Where've you been all my life?" – and is rarely sober, or solvent, again. And then there's the George Best method, whereby initial repulsion turns inexplicably to adoration to the bemusement of all – but sadly with the same ultimate end.

George, incredibly, was once a good little boy. As an Ulster teenager from a proud God-fearing family, he wasn't allowed to be anything but. The most dangerous substances he ever abused as a kid were probably the local sausages which Ulstermen fry by the pan-load every morning. But at the age of 17, George found himself in Zurich with United's youth team amidst a group of lads up for a bit of action. Best, always a suggestible kind of bloke, tagged along with them to a couple of bars, where he discovered that the Manc contingent were clearly old hands at this game, sinking pint pots on the quarter-hour with the practised manner of hardened boozers. Nothing changes, does it?

George, remarkably, had never touched a drop in his life before. And every boozer will recall the bravado of the first-timer. Once you're past that initial, utterly repellent taste, you're innocently whacking it back like water. Only when you rise for that post-second pint piss do you realise that you've stepped into the Twilight Zone. Why can't you feel your legs, and what happened to your sense of direction? After the third pint, as George desperately tried to keep up with the group drinking pace, he hit phase two – the certain knowledge that within the next 20 minutes, your guts will be on your shoes. Three questions immediately arise: where's our hotel, how are we going to get there, and what's my name again?

A taxi was the only method of escaping the watchtower which Matt and Jimmy Murphy had established in a cafe across the road from the hotel. With the right lighting and good timing, they might just be able to break back into the Stalag without the management verbally machine-gunning them from their cafe table vantage point. Poor George had half his body draped out of the window all the way back, desperately trying to swallow the bile, as the driver had told him it was double-fare for any back-seat puking.

At the entrance to the hotel, some other players managed to keep their sniggering in check in order to pull the old POW trick of surrounding a suspect man and somehow frogmarching him away from trouble. George spent the night watching the walls of his room rotate around him at 60 mph, punctuated by bouts of projectile vomiting. But at least he'd given Matt the slip, hey?

Of course, he hadn't. Matt knew only too well what young George had been up to but he guessed the episode had taught Best a lesson; he'd seen plenty of seventeen-year-olds going through the same rite of passage who'd never caused any alcohol-related problems again and he suspected Best would be the same. As did George: he told anyone who'd listen that he'd never drink again, and for several weeks he didn't. But somehow a seed of destruction had been planted. Alcohol's mysterious power called him back to try his luck with lager 'n' lime, then vodka and lemonade, and he was on his way to ruin.

1966

Between '65 and '68, George had life down pat. His drinking, shagging and football were in perfect equilibrium, the former two providing just the right amount of pressure-relief from the latter. During 1965/6, George was as much of a staple of Swinging Britain as The Beatles, but to a worldwide audience he was still just a vaguely familiar name in the odd match report. On the night of 9 March 1966, a national star became an international superstar.

United were facing the away leg of the European Cup quarter-final against the mighty Benfica, finalists from the previous season and unbeaten at home since the Jurassic era. We'd won the OT leg 3-2 but few continentals gave us an earthly: nobody could expect to carry the burden of two away goals into the frenzied cauldron of the Estadio de Luz and survive. For once, Matt eschewed his usual entreaty to "go out and enjoy yourself" and instead provided a careful plan of action: play it as tight as possible for at least 20 minutes, track back, don't get carried away in their half. If we got to half-time at 0-0, then maybe we'd still have a chance.

George had been playing quite well, but he'd only scored once since Christmas; you could probably have got at least 15-1 against him scoring first that night. A team-mate later remarked that George had appeared to be listening to Matt's talk, but that he had that familiar far-away look in his eye, the one he used to adopt in Matt's office when getting bollocked. Within 90 seconds of kick-off, it was obvious George hadn't paid a blind bit of notice. And by the twelve minute mark,

George had silenced the most fervent crowd in Europe with two goals and a display of lightning pace and supreme control that destroyed the morale of the entire Portuguese defence. Listen to any of the match commentaries from that night to hear the sound of dumbfoundment, of experienced observers unable to believe what they're seeing.

The entire team played brilliantly, of course, to win 5-1 but it was George's exhilarating bravado and flair that captured the imagination of Europe. "El Beatle" in his sombrero filled the front pages; that night, he and United had stated their footballing philosophy for the world to marvel at, and no English sporting team of any description has ever performed a greater feat abroad. The bottles and birds of the world, not just of Britain, were now open to George – but that also meant there would never be a hiding place for him again.

1968

By now, George was well into the schoolboy–headmaster aspect of his relationship with Matt. The Zurich Lesson long since forgotten, cajolings, heart-to-hearts and downright bollockings were becoming frequent occurrences between the two in Matt's office. Matt would later be criticised by the ignorant for being too soft with Best but in many ways he handled him superbly, probably extending his career by years through acting as father-confessor figure to George and offering sympathetic understanding as the world closed in around him. Best veers from guilt to boyish chuckles when he talks about these dressing-downs and it's clear he often treated them in the same fashion as he did Matt's Benfica teamtalk. He admitted that he used to pass the time while Matt lectured him by counting the animal patterns on the office wallpaper, realising on one occasion that he was really in trouble this time because he'd actually managed to count all 276 of them, such was the duration of the meeting. Sometimes he'd have to suppress his giggles as Matt tried to find gentlemanly ways to put certain incidents, especially those involving young women. Worse was when Matt tried to show how in-touch he was by citing the name of George's favourite watering hole, the Brown Bull; he could never get the name right, fulminating about the Black Bull, the Brown Cow and, at one tittersome moment, the Green Bear. Later headmasters would not be so kind or patient with Best, but the result was that they lost his services. Matt may have been indulgent but he did manage to get the best out of George, didn't he?

1969

George always wanted to win, but he took his role as an entertainer and proselytiser for beautiful football just as seriously. He never did manage to fulfill his ultimate goal – to beat an entire team, then get down on the floor and nudge the ball over the line with his head, though he did once beat the whole Blackburn reserve team from kick-off to score. But he did pull off another of his pet tricks – to score direct from a corner. Ipswich were the victims in October 1969; as the Old Trafford crowd screamed in disbelieving triumph, George trotted away grinning like the creamiest of cats. After the match, Ipswich boss Bobby Robson carped that it had been a "fluke". George fumed: how dare he impugn his skill, his commitment to the extraordinary? He had meant to do it and he had succeeded – he was an artist, not a lottery merchant. Nursing the grudge for weeks, he got his chance for revenge when United drew Ipswich in the Cup. United were awarded a corner and George hared over to take it. He struck a gorgeous, swinging yet fizzing ball which beat everyone hands-down, struck the top of the far post as intended – and then just rebounded out instead of in. Point made, nonetheless: artists display genius by design, not accident.

1970

A new decade, and a new direction for George that boded ill for the 70s. For although he'd been getting naughtier by the month, he had never yet let United down on the pitch. But on semi-final day in March 1970, as United prepared to face the old enemy Leeds, George finally got himself, and the team, scorched by burning the candle at both ends. Over lunch at their Worcester hotel, the players couldn't help noticing a rather attractive middle-class woman giving George the eye. And George was never one to duck a challenge, even though her husband was also staying at the hotel. Thirty minutes from hotel departure time, manager Wilf McGuinness used a pass key to let himself into George's room, where he found his star player going down in the box. Kick-off was less than three hours away. George was always a fit lad and a good trainer but not even he could be expected to shake off the physical exertions of a good romp. Wilf still picked him, for George was as central to the team that season as Cantona was to that of 1994, but the episode had him pulling his hair out. Worse followed. United played superbly against a Leeds side at their peak but George had a stinker. A 0-0 looked assured, when Best suddenly found himself through on the keeper. He mis-hit the ball, staggered, and collapsed ignominiously into the mud. The nearest Leeds player virtually wet himself: all the Tykes had heard about George's escapade. The game duly finished goal-less and Leeds won a disgustingly dirty second replay at Burnden Park 1-0. What might a Cup Final have done for poor Wilf and, indeed, for the whole United decade ahead? I guess George must have asked himself that too, for it remains the one incident of his United career for which he is wholly apologetic. One hopes it was a good lay because it certainly cost enough.

1975

As we'll see later, Eric Cantona's own "Magnificent Seven" involved a legendary demonstration of physical force, Clint Eastwood style. George's "Seven", no less impressive and physical, owed more to Clark Gable than Clint, as he screwed his way around Manchester in one 24-hour shagtastic marathon.

He woke up next to Number One, the previous night's pull, and started the day with a cock's crow. By lunchtime, after a pint at the Brown Bull, he was peckish: a Granada TV girl on her lunch-break filled that hole perfectly. Mid-afternoon arrives: time for something light and young between meals, so he popped off to meet the niece of some mates as she left school and helped her with her biology homework. It would have been rude to leave out the pretty young cousin staying at her flat, so when number three nipped out to the shops, George took the opportunity to keep it in family for number four. Rolling home late-afternoon, George got that horrible 5 o'clock feeling we all recognise and decided to cure it the best way he knew, by inviting round one of his regulars for a pick-me-up.

Most mortals would consider collapsing at this point but George had a night at the tables ahead of him. By the time he'd won a few quid, it had been hours since his last shag, and fortunately his date for the night was happy to oblige after he nipped into her pad for 'coffee'. Driving home with six on the card at half-four in the morning, the thought of honouring his old classic shirt number with a seventh conquest proved irresistible. Now even Bestie might have found it hard to rustle up a shag out of nothing at 4.30 in the morning, or so you might think, but it's his combination of luck, charm and savvy that makes a grade-A Lothario. He remembered the existence of a girl he barely knew who lived not too far away and decided to have a go, even though he was risking bumping into her current fella. He'd never even been out with the lass before but she let him in, in all senses of the phrase. He never saw or spoke to her again but this nameless accommodating creature had become the infamous number seven. Most blokes would have trouble physically managing seven wanks in 24 hours, let alone seven full-blown bouts of skin-surfing – and let's not even ask ourselves whether we'd ever have the pulling power to get seven to play in the first place. I guess that's why he's a Lad Legend – and why, despite all his troubles, you never need feel sorry for him.

1984

Having spent his charmed life running rings around cuck-olded husbands, harrassed managers and befuddled defenders, the law of averages dictated that he'd eventually have to come a cropper somewhere. Arrested for drink-driving in November 1984, outside Buckingham Palace of all places, he skipped the court date and became a wanted fugitive overnight. You would think that the Met, in the midst of an IRA bombing campaign, would have had better things to do yet they still managed to spare 20 bobbies to chase Best down.

Surrounded by coppers in his Chelsea flat, George bided his time until he thought they'd gone for their tea, then made a break for it out of his back window and across the road to a girlfriend's flat. As he ran, coppers sprang out from bushes, behind dustbins and unmarked cars to pounce but, as if he were still running the touchline at Old Trafford, George legged his way past and burst through his friend's door. Within minutes, the loathsome SPG had turned up too; George realised the game was up. It took eight coppers to drag him out kicking and screaming, and one cop would later charge that Best had twatted him in the face. Best, in turn, says he was beaten in the back of the van and that one cop took pleasure in hurling racist anti-Irish insults at him. George later made another dash for it when being treated by a doctor but the police were quick to pounce, one remarking that, "Mr. Best isn't quite as fast as he was, is he?" He would be sentenced to three months porridge, of which he served two, in Pentonville and Ford. The media finally had the story they'd waited a decade to report: George Best had reached rock bottom. It had been a long, winding road from that first drop of lager in Zurich to his final spirit-fuelled binge in Chelsea but there was a grim inevitability about his final destination. At least, as George shouted when they carted him out of the flat, "It took 20 of these bastards to take me!"

1990

Could George possibly embarrass himself any further than getting banged up? Yes, he could. Invited onto *Wogan* by BBC researchers who were clearly either naive or slyly cunning, George discovered the delights of the Green Room. This is the hospitality area backstage where guests are offered an array of booze – which is totally free. So to recap: the BBC takes a self-confessed alcoholic, who gets nervous on TV, and places him unsupervised amidst several open bottles of his favourite drink, wine, before sticking him in front of a live family TV audience. For once, George could argue that he was surely more sinned against than sinner.

Though not for a while yet, as the next ten minutes found George incapable of arguing anything. Fantastically glassy-eyed and lurching menacingly, George instantly alerted the watching millions that they were about to share in TV history, something that would rank alongside Ollie Reed on *After Dark* or Rod Hull's Emu on *Parkinson*. George spoke many half-sentences during his performance, none of which actually got to a full stop or linked with either what followed or preceeded them. A *tour de force* of drunken logic, complete with some "shit", "bullshit" and lots of "screwing", he reduced the supercilious Wogan to a quivering wreck, not really aided by George's attempts to stroke Terry's knee and pat his hand. In fact, it appeared as though George was revelling in the all-round humiliation, sniggering to the stunned audience that "Terry isn't sure about this, is he?" as he spewed out possibly slanderous remarks about Tommy Docherty and paeans to the pleasures of a good screw. Funny though it was, it simultaneously seemed almost unspeakably sad that the young, eloquent, sensitive man who'd appeared so impressive on *Parkinson* in 1974 had come to this.

George is on the up these days. That early 90s nadir, when he compounded the *Wogan* fiasco by making a series of deeply unpleasant remarks about Manchester United, their players and management at various sportsmen's dinners, won't be forgotten but can be forgiven. People are always forgiving

George: nowadays, it's understood that he's been the victim of a disease as much as he's been the author of his own misfortunes. The Nineties being the Decade Of The Lad, he's become a cult figure once again, with CD albums and TV theme nights dedicated to him; Sky even lets George on live TV to impart his footballing wisdom. They used to say that George would never see 40 but the chances are he'll outlive all his contemporaries, if the recent American research which claims each shag adds five minutes to you life is true. (Jeez, at that rate, he'll be outliving the as-yet unborn.) And however old he gets, it's probably safe to say that he'll still be carrying the title of the Greatest British Footballer of All-Time. And surely that of the Greatest Red Devil, too.

THE
ROCK

Jim Holton should be easy enough to describe, at least in terms of conventional wisdom: big, hard, dirty and heroic. But in reality, he's a figure surrounded by paradox and contradiction. Symbolically, The Stretford End – ever ready to twist a fact to suit a greater purpose – used to sing, "Six foot two, eyes of blue, big Jim Holton's after you", when he was actually six-one and had brown eyes. So here you have the myth of a player with "the worst United disciplinary record of all-time" – but who was actually only sent off three times, and just once in a competitive match. Here's a man who was supposedly indestructible, yet his career would be ended by injuries – sometimes innocuous ones at that – before a shockingly early death. And here was a player vilified by outsiders for being the hard, guileless face of 70s defensive bullying who ended up at a World Cup being praised for his intelligence and positional play. Nevertheless, the image lives on: Holton is now hazily remembered as a prime mid-70s ogre, the most Neanderthal of a breed recalled with both a shudder and a trace of wistful nostalgia. "They don't make 'em like Jim any-more", you'll hear: and they're right. His strain has been bred out of existence by prissy primadonnas at FIFA and UEFA, who are genetically engineering a world of football-ballet wherein the tackle from behind – one of football's greatest joys – is to be an executable offence. At least Jim played in the right era, though I imagine he'd have relished being an 1890s Heathen too.

Bred in a tough little Lanarkshire town, quite possibly on raw rams and stray Englishmen, Jim always looked like he'd been carved out of granite. With Desperate Dan jawline, mas-sive shaggy long hair and shoulders built to carry girders, his physique marked him down for only two possible roles in life: terrifying centre-half or walk-on part in a Bannockburn movie. By 1971, he might have been regretting he chose the former, as he left the Hawthorns on a free transfer without playing a single league match; Shrewsbury picked him up for a peanut wage but the career prognosis didn't look too good. Instead, within 12 months he was developing into the sensa-tion of the Third Division. Shrewsbury were crap, of course, but Jim stood above the rest both literally and figuratively. Oppo strikers soon understood that although a match with Town was generally a stroll in the country, there lurked a griz-zly bear at the heart of the defence whose cave was best avoid-ed. Smart oppos played it swift through the middle, on no account getting into a one-on-one with Holton; dullards tried Route One and got blown out of the skies by Jim's air-to-air assaults. For although Jim later became notorious for his ground-based activities, it was in the air that he made his name – a remarkably powerful jumper and battler whose sheer presence made him seem to be six foot five and sixteen stone. Put simply, any ball – or opposition skull – within

Holton Territorial Airspace was history: throughout his career, he never lost that dominance, seeing off a succession of quivering centre-forwards who soon learned not to breach Holton's sovereignty. And in an era when complaints about pampered, over-paid, semi-committed pros were just as common as they are today, there was another aspect of Jim which could not be faulted: his utter devotion to winning the ball and to putting himself at risk in so doing if required. Had the adjective existed then, the only fitting description would have been Robsonian.

As 1973 arrived, there was one team above all who needed some blood 'n' guts in their defence – Manchester United. A byword since their 60s heyday for back four frailty and defensive lapses, United now looked Titanically holed below the waterline at the back as they fought relegation. There was no point in having the smooth Captain Buchan on deck without sufficient burly deck-hands alongside him to stop United shipping goals. Say one thing for Docherty: he knew his lower division rough diamonds. Whilst acquiring notoriety for his megabuck big-name buys early on, Docherty's £80,000 purchase of Holton would prove to be the first in a succession of canny below-stairs acquisitions, Third Class steerage punters coming up to First and putting such bumbling aristocrats as George Graham and Mick Martin to shame. Jim's Scottish blood had secured him a spot on the Doc short-list from the moment the new manager arrived, and Tommy's Nietzschean vision of a team stuffed with master race Tartan duly took effect. As Germany '74 hove into view, half of Scotland's team would soon be plucked from Old Trafford's ranks – incredibly, Jim would be one of them, having rocketed from West Brom reject to potential world star within a couple of years.

Such a prospect looked laughably improbable on 20

January 1973 when Jim stepped out onto Old Trafford's turf for his Red debut and proceeded to scare the shit out of his own supporters, rather than the opposition strikers. Whilst Lou Macari made a dream start upfront, Jim caused jaws to drop for rather different reasons at the other end. Stretford Enders were used to desperation, of course. O'Farrell had only been sacked four weeks before and United were in the middle of eight games without a win, apparently plummetting towards Division Two. That day, Reds were watching some leading low-lights of the living dead brigade – George Graham, Ted MacDougall, Wyn Davies, Tony Young – so at least a disastrous debutant had somewhere to hide. Jim was partly to blame for both Hammers goals (United recovered to draw 2-2) but it was the nature of his groundwork that amazed. Sure, the pitch has never been worse than it was that month, even more threadbare and bumpy than 1992's. But Jim's treatment of the ball on the ground as a completely alien object, to be watched, maybe scuffed at, but never properly kicked, horrified the more cultured observers. Hammers darted gleefully about him like speedboats around a tanker.

Holton's response to his exposure as someone who, to say the least, needed to work on his timing across the ground, was typical. He got stuck in, with both sets of studs. 59,000 who crammed in to see United draw 0-0 with Everton witnessed the birth of a legend. To be honest, he still didn't play very well in pure football terms. But then to judge Jim solely on such terms was to miss the point. What he showed most of all was an almost manic desire not to be beaten, as though losing a ball would be a stain on his Scottish ancestry. Reds hadn't seen much of this attitude lately and began to bay in appreciation. The team were now in hard 4-4-2 formation, clearly playing tighter and tougher. Scousers were getting kicked all

J. BANNISTER,

A. BELL,

H. BURGESS,

R. DUCKWORTH,

W. MEREDITH,

C. ROBERTS,

A. TURNBULL,

J. TURNBULL,

G. WALL,

The Outcasts FC – Man Utd's militant Red Devils circa 1907 – led both on and off the field by the mighty Billy Meredith and Alex 'Sandy' Turnbull

Left: You dirty Barson –
fearless Frank, the original
footballing hardman

Back Row (left to right) : J. Carey, J. Anderson, J. Crompton, A. Chilton, H. Cockburn, J. Aston.
Front Row : J. Delaney, J. Morris, J. Rowley, S. Pearson, C. Mitten.

Above: Old Trafford's immediate post World War II line up including
'cheeky' Charlie Mitten (front row, far right) soon to be the Bogota
bandit

Georgie Boy pulls another pint

Big Jim Holton, another of Docherty's tartan signings, plies his brutal
trade in a 70s encounter with the Auld Enemy

Paddy Roche closes his eyes and miraculously finds the ball in his hands. Not United's best keeper

Tommy Doc checks the FA Cup's hallmark during his Wembley lap of honour in 1977

Mickey Thomas – the counterfeit winger

Dieu among Diables, the kung fu king shows an early aptitude for secret ninja hand signals

over the park. And Jim was putting it about more than anyone. So maybe his timing was off, his positional radar still set
to Division Three standards, his tackling rudimentary (and
the ref missed the most blatant penalty offence). So what? He
was compensating with extraordinary passion and effort, and
a novel tackling technique not seen at OT in decades.
Essentially, he combined the almost nasty unyielding tigerish-
ness of Stiles and Crerand with the physical force and aggres-
sion of a Barson: the result, euphemistically decribed in the
press as a "jarring" or "shuddering" challenge, was more akin
to a war movie scene on turf. Holton was the Panzer, the poor
sod on the receiving end the plywood shack. The Stretford
End loved it and a cult hero was born.

As I always like to point out, the idea that United fans only
idolise artistes like Charlton, Best and Giggs is a total fallacy.
How easily outsiders forget that we also venerated the likes of
Whiteside, Stiles and Holton himself, and that the notion of
United as a showman's club is very much a post-war con-
struct. And when times are hard, as they were in '73, the last
thing you want to see are inconsistent fancy Dans fannying
about à la George Graham. You want fighters, hardmen,
bleeders – men like Jim Holton.

Not that Jim was intentionally dirty, at least not in the cynical way often imputed to certain Leeds United personnel of
the era. Apocryphal story (with a bitter aftertaste, in hindsight): Mrs Holton says to neighbour she's "worried Jim will
come home with a broken leg". Neighbour says, "Don't worry,
it won't be his." That's told about several particular legendary
hardmen, all of whom had one thing in common – an absence
of premeditated malice. The worst you could say about Jim was
that he could be reckless in regard to consequences, like a
drunk driver in charge of a bulldozer. His, um, 'idiosyncratic'

timing could sometimes make his full-blooded charges look like attempted GBH but in truth it was more a case of him simply being a bit unwillingly late rather than wantonly lethal. Indeed, I can't recall him breaking anyone else's leg, yet he broke his own twice; that generous-spirited sharing of the risk is telling, and one that was absent from the careers of notorious assassins like Tardelli, for example. They called Jim many things in his career – monster, horror, barbarian – but never assassin. He was hard, but honest, prepared to pay the price for his own physicality. And by never shirking a challenge or pulling a punch, he was one of those rare players who never, for a moment, cheated the punter. In '74's fight to the death, there was no "saving something for Germany" bollocks with Jim: it remained kick or be kicked until the trapdoor swung open.

By the middle of March 1973, Holton had already assured himself a place in United fans' collective memory. During one mental week in February, he achieved what was once seen as impossible by getting sent off in a friendly at Porto, before coming home to trounce England's silkiest player John Richards when Wolves came to OT, stunning fans with some – gulp – ball-playing skill. One paper dragged out the Jekyll and Hyde analogy but it was really all of a piece: he just didn't like getting beaten by anyone or anything. And if that meant, at this level, learning to play on the ground a bit, he'd do the crash course. Pundits marvelled at his progress from raw Third Division beast to, erm, raw International beast; indeed, few players have come to Old Trafford and tackled a steep learning curve quite so quickly and successfully as Jim. Nevertheless, thank God for 70s refereeing standards, for rarely did ten minutes go by without Jim giving some wretched oppo the kind of clobbering that would today bring instant dismissal. In those days, the striker in question usually had no option but to get up and get on with it – today, they'd be screaming for ambulances, lawyers and ten-match bans. Occasionally, Reds would have the extra treat of seeing him come up against an equally ogrish figure – Leeds's Joe Jordan springs to mind – to produce 90 minutes of X-rated skull-crashing intensity which would rise like sulphurous steam from the pitch. By the end of the '72/3 season, Jim was entrenched, fittingly granite-like, in the heart of United's first-choice line-up, feted by many as one of the main reasons United had survived the drop. He'd even popped upfield and scored three goals (one during the infamous Newcastle match which saw him also receive his only competitive red card), offensive forays which terrified oppo defenders who'd normally thank their lucky stars that they weren't condemned to play upfront against him. With Jim on board, surely '73/4 could only be better?

The bitter irony would be that, in the very season when United looked defensively stronger than at any time since '68, it would be our mythical attacking prowess that would let us down. Jim Holton won the '73/4 United Player of the Year award, and his partnership with Buchan was many pundits' choice for the best in the division, but our miserable goals-scored haul of 38 condemned us to Division Two. Even at the very height of his playing powers, which duly guaranteed his slot in the Scottish World Cup side, Jim remained every outsider's favourite target. When United lost at Spurs in November, during a month in which we played well but found ourselves win-less, Jim snapped in rage at Mike England and got stuck into a hugely amusing punch-up. Naturally, this only served to endear him still further to the travelling Red Army but the media rounded on him, citing him as the prime example of the ugly new face of United. Armchair critics griped about United's dirtiness, their abandonment of carefree attacking football, their willingness to get into the gutter and slug it out when provoked. Quite rightly, Martin Buchan led the counter-attack, pointing out that when you're fighting for your lives and the only decent part of your team is the defence, what other option could you take? Jim charged on, unfazed, roaring defiance until that last horrendous April Waterloo. There was dishonour in United's relegation, to be sure, but not a drop of it tainted Holton. Still, the union of First Division strikers was mighty glad to see the back of him.

The Holton tragedy was that he never got the chance to come back and terrorise his auld enemies again. As he and Buchan torched all before them in Division Two, thrilling the well-established Jim Holton Fan Club whose newsletter proudly reported his latest striker-destroying escapades, nemesis was only weeks away. In front of the Battle of Hillsborough on 7 December 1974, as thousands refought the War of the Roses on the terraces, Jim Holton broke his leg. Poetic justice to some, but the darkest moment of the season to every Red. It had been an almost surreal afternoon, the teams contriving a 4-4 classic amidst chaotic crowd scenes that were extraordinary even for the mid-70s; that Jim Holton could be physically damaged by anything short of a Scud seemed incredible. But grievously harmed he was: it had been a bad break, and it seemed to shatter the aura of invincibility that had always surrounded Jim.

It took him half a year to fight back to fitness but then, in a pre-season friendly against Red Star, he slipped on the ball and somehow put himself out of action yet again. Why was it always friendlies and reserve games that gave him aggravation?

A cosmic mismatch, perhaps – Holton was the kind of player you felt was demeaned by playing in anything other than 110 per cent commitment first-team crunch matches. "Holton"and "friendly" ought not to appear in the same footballing sentence. So typically, it would be a comeback reserve match a few weeks later that witnessed the final blow: another broken leg, and this one left him a broken player.

Jim slipped out of Old Trafford under cover of the hype surrounding the Ajax–United match in October '76. He'd played against Huddersfield for our reserves the previous Monday but Docherty had decided he'd never quite make the top grade again. Just before he left, to play out a career twilight at Sunderland and Coventry amongst others, United had secured a 2-2 draw up at St. James's Park in precisely the kind of match that Jim always loved. A windswept rainstorm blew across the Toon all day and the twenty-two players had knocked rather more than seven bells out of each other, in apparent synchronicity with warring rival fans on the terraces. "Footballers aren't fairies," Doc had snorted afterwards when it was suggested that it had been a tough day. Not quite so true today, but then there are no Jim Holtons around to terminate them anymore, are there?

Jim had retired happily to the Midlands where he ran a popular pub, always a stop-over for Reds on their travels. He died suddenly, and somehow unbelievably, at the age of 42: the hardest, toughest United player in living memory, yet injuries and accident had ended his career and his life with shocking prematurity. Irony at its grimmest; but amongst United fans of a certain age, he'll be much missed and always fondly remembered as one of the Reddest of Dirty Devils.

THE
GREEN-DYED
MONSTER

Like many football fans whose ideals were formed in the 1970s, I spend a lot of time moaning about goalkeepers – or specifically, how pampered they are these days. Breathe on one from six yards and you're off, or so it seems; certainly, dare to challenge him properly for a cross and you get Bob Wilson screaming outrage into the nearest mike. And what a cushy life they have professionally too: they hardly have to be at the cutting edge of peak fitness, and a Man United goalie in particular can look forward to doing nothing more stamina-draining in some home games than pick his nose for 88 minutes. Or shout obscenities at our centre-backs, if they're the Danish variety. Moreover, they can then trundle on as players until they're 87, or whatever age Peter Shilton is these days, whilst the outfield likes of Giggs and Co. face burn-out at 30. All that may be true but there's a price to pay in the Faustian goalkeeper's pact. For his isolated position puts him in unique jeopardy when it comes to bad form. Your average workhorse midfielder can hide in the engine room for weeks and run it off (or not, in Brian McClair's case). Even your star striker can seemingly survive months of bollocking around the box *à la* Birtles, Cole or Sheringham because for some reason we never quite exactly equate the bad miss with the goalkeeping blunder, do we? You could argue that between 1995 and 1997 Andy Cole's cock-ups cost United at least 20 goals and numerous points, yet there we were in the midst of '97/98 singing three different Andy Cole songs. But dress in green (or whatever ridiculous colour Umbro's dictating that month) and let in a handful of soft ones and you're never forgiven.

Deep down, I suspect most of us subconsciously dislike goalkeepers. It probably stems from the playground, when crap kids were sent into the net as punishment for their ineptitude. Or is it that the utter centrality of the goal-scoring act in football, the orgasm at the end of a passing move's foreplay, inculcates in us a subliminal detestation of any goalkeeping *coitus interruptus*? Even when we have as heroic and successful a guardian as the Viking Peter, don't you ever suspect that he is still under-rated, or at least under-celebrated, when he should by rights be acknowledged as the key to our 90s domination?

So goalies are easy to pick on. In a way, because they're semi-detached from the team, it doesn't feel as disloyal to the cause to slag the 'keeper. And whereas you always used to be able to defend Cole by blaming the chance-suppliers for not delivering precisely the right kind of ball, a goalie can only get so far by blaming the defence. When the shot finally comes in and he fumbles it into the net, there's no-one else to point the finger at; as others have remarked, goalkeeping is the existentialist's favourite position, where you live or die as a result of your own, sole, free-willed choice. Albert Camus, as it happens, was an excellent keeper. Paddy Roche, however, was not.

It was the autumn of 1975 and the world looked upon

Docherty's thrilling kids as genuine title contenders – and handily placed in the League Cup too, thanks to a smart, well-paced third round win at Villa. But that was October. In November, Paddy Roche trotted out onto the pitch; by the 22nd, his efforts had seemed to ensure that United would not be troubling the Football League medal-forgers on either count. Three cataclysmic performances at Anfield, Maine Road and Highbury revealed him to be a monstrous bogey-man for every young Red's nightmares. A recent *Red Issue* contributor wrote of how his bedroom walls were then plastered with United team pics; on every one, Paddy's face had been scrawled out with blunt implements. Today, people can laugh and sing ironic songs about 80s disaster Ralphie Milne. But Roche's name will forever go unsung.

A £15,000 buy from Shelbourne in '73, Roche didn't even look like a goalkeeper. Awkward, gangly, small and beetle-browed, he looked more suited to ticket office work. But as he waited on the sidelines for his big chance, watching United roar back up to Division One throughout 1975, he must have had an inkling that his time would definitely be coming. Docherty, bar one enquiry for Shilton, had shown no interest in other new keepers, and his relationship with Alex Stepney was going down the pan. Stepney was an endangered breed at OT – a Busby loyalist and therefore on Doc's ultimate hitlist, and a man who spoke his mind in the dressing room. Docherty had already told him as '75/6 kicked off that he was living on borrowed time; when Roche was finally elevated to the first team, it was supposed to herald a permanent switch. Within two weeks of Roche's quiet debut against Norwich, both press and fans were howling for Stepney's return and, in the Stretford End's case, for Roche's convenient dismemberment in some dark Salford alleyway.

It was typical of Paddy's wretched luck that fate should have chosen Anfield as the place to reveal his true nature to us. Here was your classic four-pointer between Championship contenders, with the burgeoning Scouse–Manc common hatred forming an extra spicey ingredient. As 6,000 Reds groaned behind their Anfield Road steel partition, Roche cost us the game with dazzling cock-ups for the scousers' first and third goals. That first goal, when even the fans could hear Greenhoff shout, "Leave it!", only to see Roche come barging out into collision before dropping the ball into the path of a stunned Scouser, set the tone for the fortnight. Objectively, it was a hilarious sight; subjectively, it felt like the Grim Reaper had arrived to set up shop in the heart of our title challenge. The press raved about the entertainment that afternoon but United could hardly do anything other than attack full-pelt given the disarray behind them. Kevin Keegan, at his most smarmy and patronising afterwards, lauded United for the way they played, doubtless slyly realising that any more such kamikaze awaydays could hand the dull Scousers the title.

Paddy, however, was quite capable of wrecking United's hopes in more than just one competition. Four days later, we were due at Maine Road for a fourth round League Cup tie which Red Manchester had been salivating over for five weeks. Bear in mind that it had been over 12 years since United played in a domestic Cup Final of any sort; there was none of the Wembley-*ennui* we get today, but a grasping desperation to go one better than we had in '74/5 and reach the Final. More importantly, the Mancunian throne awaited. After several years in City's shadows, at least in terms of trophy achievement and derby results, this team was mounting a counter-revolution. We were, at last, ahead of them in the League and if we got through this round, it would be the first time since the Sixties that we'd survived three derbies in a row unbeaten. We would thus, once again, be undisputed cocks of the walk.

City played well that night, there's no denying it. But not well enough *per se* to justify inflicting upon us the worst derby scoreline since the 50s. No, for that extra mile they needed the services of Paddy. It wasn't just that he was at fault for two of the four goals City cracked past us that night, errors that in any event were not quite as glaring as those perpetrated at Anfield. Rather it was his general behaviour that mortified, undermining the fabric of the defence and the team like some dementedly over-excited breed of termite. You could have sworn that he was actually shaking with fear as he fannied about his six-yard box – and it wasn't that cold a night, despite the rain – and all you could hope for was that his defenders didn't catch sight of him too often as he grimaced and twitched and skulked through the ninety. He had all the goal-mouth presence of a fart in a canyon. That morning after in the schoolyard was the worst of my pre-teen life and I, for one, knew whom to blame. So, it seemed, did the rest of the Red tribes.

Finally, there was Arsenal away, never a venue we enjoyed at the best of times, which these were not. In the '70s, Arsenal were somehow bigger rivals than they are today. A combination of surging Cockney Red influence, the bad temper of some of the clashes and the terrace aggro that was always guaranteed placed Highbury up with Maine Road, Anfield and Elland Road as a major trip of the season. You begin to see, don't you, the unique power of the Roche legend – that he should perform his anti-heroics at three of our four most important rivals' grounds within a 14-day period?

With much of the pre-match publicity centering on the

Roche Question – and with Docherty giving quite the wrong answer by claiming he'd stick with him – it was no wonder the Gunners looked even more confident than usual about their chances of extending United's Highbury hoodoo. In fact, they couldn't wait to get near our box and have a go. Twelve seconds gone and we're one-down. Despite McIlroy's injury and the nerve-jangling state of the defenders in front of Roche, we fight back. Pearson's cracking volley takes us to 1-2; with a minute to go United are looking for the break, roared on by an especially vocal United contingent. Just as we're hoping to tidy up from a corner and launch an equalising assault, Roche performs a trick of unparalleled timing and awfulness: *he punches into his own goal.* Cheers, jeers and laughter combine to hoot us out of Highbury, our title challenge surely fatally holed, and a hundred Irish goalkeeper jokes are born to give the poor Scots a break.

After such a catalogue of infamy a keeper at, say, Grampus 8 would surely have immediately retired to the dressing room with his favourite ceremonial sword and a bowl to catch his intestines. Unbelievably, Roche didn't get run out of town but was to return to the team one day; for the time being, however, Docherty had no option but to bow to the howls of derision and reinstate Stepney. Poor Paddy: probably a nice guy, did his best, just happened to make a lifetime's worth of errors in 14 days against three of our four most hated opponents in crucial, honours-deciding games. "Happens all the time, son," says Mrs Leighton. In his book years later, Sammy McIlroy couldn't help himself: "If we hadn't conceded those goals, we'd have won the title", he bluntly reflected.

Paddy has joined the ranks of the Old Trafford immortals, in one way: he's one of those very few players, like David May in Gothenberg or Andy Cole at Upton Park, at whom you can point and say, "He cost us that trophy." May and Cole have at least partially redeemed themselves, of course, by later producing trophy-clinching moments themselves. Paddy never got such a chance – when Dave Sexton remarkably gave him two further small runs in the team in 1977 and 1978, United's chances of winning any trophy bar Most Mental Fans Award seemed remote to say the least. And even though his further spells never featured quite the catastrophic concentration of his epic '75 residency, he still managed to play a leading part in some horrendous afternoons: the 0-4 home humiliation by Forest in '77/8; the *déjà vu* 1-3 at Anfield two months later; and my personal 'favourites', the utter embarrassments that were the 1-3 and 1-5 reverses against Bristol City and Birmingham in '78/9. That last defeat fittingly marked the end of his last proper run in United colours – Gary Bailey arrived to rescue us a week later. Roche staggered on in the Reserves, surely his more natural home, until we finally managed to offload him to Brentford in 1982. You could almost feel sorry for him: nine years' faithful service at the Club, yet he's solely remembered for 270 minutes' work in November 1975, a memory enduring enough 22 years later to get him into the pages of *Red Issue*'s Worst United XI Of All Time feature. Cruel and unfair perhaps, but like I said – deep down, we're never happier than when blaming goalkeepers.

Which is why, as a postscript a decade later, we 'enjoyed' more of this unique sado-masochistic weirdness with Jim Leighton. Stereotypical assumptions run deep on terraces, and the prospect of a Scottish goalkeeper – however expensive – never did make the heart sing. For the best part of five years, as we easily forget nowadays, our collective terrace wisdom was that in a stadium of 45,000, there were 44,999 better judges of a player than Alex Ferguson. Remember as late as

April 1990 Fergie defending Jim as "the best keeper in Scotland", as if that was supposed to be a clinching, soothing argument?

Leighton was a lynching waiting to happen, if we're honest. His appearance didn't help, making Roche look quite imposing by comparison – that overbite was pure Simpsons (cf. the episode featuring the convict babysitter) and the bandy legs equally cartoonish. It didn't take much to imagine a ball whizzing through between his knees as he tries in vain to keep his legs together. And he was such a miserable-looking mutha too, about as inspirational to fans and defenders as a funeral; when it was later pointed out that he looked suicidal on the sidelines during the 1990 Cup replay, the reply was, "How can you tell?"

His powers, such as they were, drained away gradually after he joined us. His was not an initial explosion of crappery like Roche's but something more akin to bowel disease – slow, painful, and virtually inoperable. There was a classic early cock-up against Southampton in '88/9, caught by TV, when he skewered a harmless high ball into the net when alone in the box but this was simply a warning shot. He accumulated bad notices incrementally, and grew steadily before you into a disaster as you watched over several months. By the middle of '89/90, as United scrabbled around at the foot of the table, the terrace knives came out into the open as the collective realisation dawned that Son Of Paddy was amongst us. *Red Issue* led a vociferous "Leighton Out!" campaign, climaxing in the distribution of T-shirts featuring the notorious Leighton Condom cartoon: "Guaranteed to catch nothing – shoot with confidence" ran the shout-line, next to an indelible image of Jim as a human sheath. You knew Leighton's cause was lost when a couple of United players asked for the mail-order details. Those remaining public loyalists, all apparently sharing the address "c/o The Manager's Office", who argued that fans were wrecking his confidence were frankly closing doors after bolted horses. This nag was heading for the knackers' yard, and everyone knew it.

One time-served Red I know seriously cites the greatest moment of his pre-marital life as this: standing on his Wembley seat overlooking the tunnel before the Cup Final replay and seeing Les Sealey in the goalkeeper's jersey. Leighton's flapping on the Saturday which had cost us two goals in front of laughing millions worldwide had, at last, been a blunder too far. The campaign had succeeded, and Leighton's career south of the border was dead. He would spend much of the next few years savaging Fergie for his treachery (*sic*), before supposedly proving us all wrong with a Scottish renaissance. As a good review in the Scottish League is about as useful as the Pope's balls, I think it's safe to say that few Reds have ever regretted his departure for a millisecond. Yet, somehow, Paddy still looms larger in the nightmares for anyone over 30.

THE
DOC

When The Doc was called to tend to the sickness at United after Frank O'Farrell's 1972 sacking, a 70s archetype replaced the last of the 60s gents. Poor Frank – can O'Farrell ever be mentioned without a sympathetic prefix? – always appeared to belong to a former era. Those awful pictures showing Frank with stern expression, plastered-down hair and ramrod tie seem to come from the same time-frozen stock as those iconic snaps of Ian Brady and Lord Lucan. His manner placed him alongside Cullis, Nicholson and Ramsey in a world of clenched buttocks, stiff lips and correct behaviour. Frank did everything above board and by the book whereas Docherty didn't know where the book was and virtually lived under the table. A 70s Old Trafford was surely no place for an O'Farrell – but it was made for The Doc, 70s Man incarnate. Put him in a kipper tie, in *Man About The House*, next to a Party Seven or behind the wheel of a Capri – does he not fit perfectly within your mental image? Now try the same with poor Frank...see what I mean? Faced with the svelte Paula Wilcox,

Frank would surely have told her to put some less indecent clothes on, leaving The Doc to hide Cup Final tickets down her bra and ask if she fancied some horizontal training.

To take on the shambles at United in December 1972 required some sly, brash, courageous, savvy, charming and brutal flair; and whatever your opinion of the Doc as a person, manager or court-room witness, he was the ideal man for the moment. If the footballing 60s were dead, then so too were the concomitant integrity, gentlemanly codes, correct reserve and modest rewards: for the cynical, flash, hardbitten and loudly moneyed 70s, United had a man who understood his era to take the helm. (Naturally, this has its risks, as United were to discover: like the live TV show which invited the Sex Pistols on, anticipating a viewing figures bonanza, you can't complain when they turn round and shout, "Dirty fucker!" at the screen. It goes with the territory. So scarred were United by their own Johnny Rotten that they were to appoint his absolute opposite as successor.)

Conventional wisdom at the time was that the Doc's short Scotland managerial assignment in '71 had been the making of him, giving him the required gravitas for United, not to mention nurturing his insatiable taste for buying anyone who'd ever been near tartan underwear. Back in the mid-60s, this Seventies Man archetype had actually tried the authoritarian, straight-laced and hands-off approach of an O'Farrell; a mad night out in Blackpool by Venables and his Chelsea cohorts signalled the beginning of the end of that tactic. As the decade turned his burgeoning reputation for, um, 'eccentricity' grew. Yet the meandering drift through the wastelands of Rotherham, Villa, Hull, QPR and Oporto were to be forgiven: that so few laughed out loud when the Doc was linked to United demonstrated just how far he'd been rehabilitated.

New bosses at OT are expected to trot out the usual cliches: "This is the finest club in the land", "These fans are the greatest", "I am here for the honour not the money (though thanks for the 50% hike and flash car)", "Every player here will get a good chance to show me what he can do." The Doc duly conformed, but demurred from the fourth. He had, it seemed, made his mind up long since. Later he would talk of approaching the job with scalpel in hand – they had called the Doc so he was ready for surgery. Docherty talked of the "cancer" and "canker" within, mixing metaphors to add "dead wood"; lumberjack or butcher, the Doc was about to start cutting.

When Docherty talked of "dead wood" and "cancers", he had King Denis Law in mind more than most. He held that Denis had "stopped trying", that he spent "four days a week on the treatment table", that "all he cared about was how long he could continue playing." The scalpel was ready for a final surgery, without anaesthetic.

In early 1973, as the Doc began to negotiate his way around Old Trafford's political minefields, he took to dining with the Crerands and Laws – a Fifth Columnist operating in the midst of a Busbyite mafia (*sic*) perhaps. Whatever information Docherty gained from people he would later characterise as the enemy, he foolishly gave up a hostage to fortune – in front of witnesses, offering Denis a "job for life" on more than one occasion. No surprise in that: half-a-dozen Busby Boys had ended up on the payroll post-retirement. Denis, who didn't want to leave the Club or become a fully-fledged manager, was delighted. Here was the reassurance every loyal thirty-something player wants to hear, the promise of a kind of footballing private pension-hood.

Later, Docherty would deny ever having given such assurances: "How could I promise a job for life when I only had a contract for three years myself?", he claimed sophistically.

27 April 1973. Bobby's about to get the full-colours career burial next day at Chelsea and Denis knows he'll enjoy a similar tear-jerking ceremony sometime in the next year or so. He gambols through training in wide-eyed innocence, completely unaware that Docherty has been to the Board to secure a free transfer for him – only Busby himself objected. As Law heads for home, Tommy calls him into the office to hand over what Denis himself termed "a sentence of death".

Somehow, despite the shock of seeing promises smashed before his eyes, Denis found the presence of mind to cobble together a compromise on the spot. If he couldn't have the future he'd been assured, or even just another season as a player, then at least he could stagger on towards his testimonial, keeping his public dignity and reputation. Docherty agreed: Law could remain a player and announce his retirement from football on the day of his testimonial, which was only four months away after all. The two old warriors had saved face, as important to Scots as to Japanese samurai. If Law had been unwillingly shafted – which he undoubtedly had – then at least it had been in the dark, with lubrication and a condom. The world outside would only see a royal abdication in August, with the full pomp and circumstance. No-one would know of Docherty's scheme or Law's disappointment.

Saturday lunchtime. Denis is in an Aberdeen pub, surrounded by friends and well-wishers as ever. *Football Focus*, babbling from a telly above the bar, announces curtly that Law and Tony Dunne have been dumped by Docherty on freebies. Denis tries hard in his book to explain how hard this fist smashing into his emotional solar plexus hurt: adjectives fail him. The last vestiges which Docherty had left him to cover his nakedness were ripped away in seconds. For Law, this was treachery of an unforgiveable sort.

Law hared back to Manchester in frantic search of an explanation and a culprit, which was the only consolation on offer. The damage couldn't be repaired, of course. If this hadn't been Docherty's doing, to suspend disbelief for a moment, then a prompt denial from Tommy within the hour might've done the trick. By the time Denis reached Manchester, no such statement had materialised. Docherty later suggested that the news could've been leaked by Law's dining partners, or even indirectly by Sir Matt himself. To what end would that have been? As a defence, it was about as credible as OJ's. Docherty's own silence in the wake of the report was rather more convincing to this jury. When he himself admitted he "might have let it slip to David Meek or someone like that", the ring of truth sounded. This was more like the Docherty of legend, shooting from the hip around town to any who'd listen and not caring overmuch whom his stray bullets struck.

Denis was told at Old Trafford that "pressure from the media" had forced the release of the news. "That explanation wasn't worth two bob – according to my agreement reached with Tommy, there should have been no news to release", judged Denis. Docherty's own 1981 version leaves a gaping hole at this point – he simply doesn't address it. Perhaps he's learned one thing from his legal tribulations after all; sometimes, rather than incriminate yourself through verbal contortion and evasion, it's better to keep schtum. Suddenly, the image of a New York *consigliere* growling, "I'm taking the Fifth," comes to mind.

Denis took his free, went to City and proved a couple of points to Docherty in a painfully forceful way. And if Law was the first notable victim of the Docherty Treatment, he wouldn't be the last. It's a pity for Docherty that he didn't share his successor's interest in Oriental maxims: he might then have recalled "Be careful lest you make too many enemies on the way up – they'll all be there to help you on your way down."

With Law and Charlton disposed of, only one European Footballer of the Year remained to be discarded. George Best has memorised what he claims Docherty said to him when he rejoined United in '73 and he'll repeat it verbatim whenever asked: "If you have a night out and miss training, you'll have to come back and do it in the afternoon. But no-one will ever know about it. It will remain between you and me – I promise you." The test, eventually, came in the week of United's January '74 cup-tie with Plymouth. George, for the first time since September, missed training on the Wednesday morning. Anxious to keep his word, he did the extra stint that afternoon; no-one said a word about it to him for the next two days and, for George, the matter was forgotten. A mistake made but immediately repaired – hadn't that been the deal? Clearly, the lessons of the Law Affair hadn't been fully learned by this particular player...

Saturday match-day. The Doc has told the players to report to the Grill Room at 11.30. And on this much, it is agreed: Georgie didn't roll up at the ground until 2.30. But then, that had always been the Best way. If Sir Matt had accepted it, why not lesser men? Docherty now says he took Best aside into the ref's room and told him he was being dropped for his lateness – and for not being in a fit state to play, accusing Best of having had a lunchtime drop or two. (Better a Best with a double inside him than a completely sober Mick Martin, you might suggest.) No-one else who saw Best before kick-off has suggested he was even vaguely pissed, however. Docherty also claims now that Best simply wasn't up to it anymore, that his comeback had failed on football terms. Yet he picked Best throughout the period and had him down to play that cup-tie; clearly at this point he was deemed good enough for a Doc team.

You may, therefore, find Best's version rather more persuasive. Especially in the light of the mysterious leak to Thursday's press that Best had missed training. For by Saturday, the tabloid blood-sport zealots had hyped up a triviality into a trial of strength between Docherty and Best. Once again, the Cantona comparison comes to mind: how a minor foul becomes evidence of near psychotic outbreak when translated by the *Sun*. The jackals wanted to see Best slapped down, humiliated; no secret pact between the Doc and George could survive such pressure. Best remembers his version of the 2.30 confrontation: "Docherty said he wasn't playing me. I asked why. 'Because you didn't turn up for training.' 'But I came in on the afternoon as we agreed.' Docherty said it didn't matter: 'I can't let it be seen that you are bigger than me.' Tommy Docherty had lied to me."

This, then, was the Best variation of the Docherty Treatment. George refused all further peace offers, perhaps in the heat of the moment but also on principle. Because as far as he was concerned, "Docherty was a liar" – and he wouldn't work for a man who didn't have integrity, in whom he couldn't place his own trust. Perhaps George had been spoiled by having had Sir Matt to believe in and to rely upon, leaving him unsuited for the grim machinations of most other managerial regimes – and certainly of this one.

It would be the removal of the poor man's George Best that'd finally undo the Doc. November 1974 – and there's a couple of different Willie Morgan song mixes doing the rounds. On the Stretford, it still goes: "Hey hey, clear the way, here comes Willie Morgan / Willie, Willie Morgan on the wing" etc. etc. But out in a Manchester pub, frequented by a certain roly-poly semi-cut Scot, they allegedly prefer: "Willie Morgan on the wing / He's a cunt, I'm gonna sort him out / He'll be on the way out / Before the end of the season." And so he was: what a coincidence, hey?

Yet Morgan and Docherty had once been, um, thick as thieves. Willie recommended Tommy for the managerial job and praised him lavishly even when we went down. Tommy dubbed him "the world's greatest right-winger" and sealed the membership of their mutual admiration society by making him captain. And thereby hangs a tale which twisted all the way to the Old Bailey.

During the summer of '74, Morgan detached a retina playing tennis, a serious injury for a sportsman who relies on limb/ball/eye co-ordination. Docherty played the solicitous boss to perfection but Morgan soon felt more like Boxer in *Animal Farm*, a stalwart seen as damaged goods who'd be carted off to the glue factory on the slightest excuse. By late autumn, Morgan was the team scapegoat, the one who'd always get hauled off first and bad-mouthed off the record. Whispers around town echoed back to Morgan – Tommy was marking his cards, pronouncing death threats through the bottom of a glass or even singing them from a table-top. By January, Morgan was no longer captain; by March, his obvious heir apparent had arrived from Tranmere. Even if it were true, as Docherty alleged, that Morgan's eyesight was failing, here was some writing on the wall which even Willie could read.

Still, as with Law, he hardly deserved what was coming. Docherty maintained Morgan had spent virtually the whole season asking for a transfer though perhaps that was just wishful thinking: certainly, Morgan would probably take anyone who suggested this was the case to court. And, with a six-year deal and forthcoming testimonial in the back pocket, Morgan would surely have been a real footballing rarity to have looked for the exit, at least until Coppell's arrival. The Board minutes show Docherty reporting as early as October '74 that Morgan was asking for a move but that he as manager was nobly resisting him. Come May, with Morgan showing no sign of wanting to accept the loaded revolver in a quiet back room, a touch of the Law treatment was clearly required.

Tellingly, Docherty skips this bit in his 1981 book. Morgan, however, told Jim White: " Tommy came to me and said, 'I want us to be friends. Don't come on the Far East tour – take the family on a club holiday and I'll see you when I get back.' The next thing I see is the front page of the *Manchester Evening News*: MORGAN REFUSES TO GO ON TOUR."

Tommy had secured the end-game; a couple of smart moves later, he'd pushed Morgan into checkmate and Willie was on his way to Burnley for thirty grand. Another Busbyite knight off the board – another enemy for life acquired. In June 1977, Morgan appeared on Granada TV one teatime. Bristling with righteous anger and burning with unrequited vengeance, he revelled in Docherty's imminent downfall. "He's about the worst manager there's ever been and nearly all United fans will be delighted when he goes," he declared. A month later, a writ for libel from Docherty's brief arrived. Suddenly, a new kind of end-game was on offer. And to switch match metaphor for a moment, this time "Willie Morgan On The Wing" would be replaced (as you'll see) by Morgan as a fully-armed and very pissed-off lethal centre-forward.

Tommy's own Kids weren't immune from the Doc

Treatment either, as they discovered during United's 1975 summer tour. Like many of United's 70s foreign excursions – St. Etienne, Tehran, Porto – this slog around the Far East did not appear to have been planned with much *savoir faire*. It turned out to be a long, tiring, sweaty and bad-tempered haul; worse, it was done on the cheap. Grouchy players and management staggered onto Australia, a battleground simply waiting for a spark.

The touring party assembled in a hotel function room for what looked like a clear-the-air meeting, a description which proved to be a touch inappropriate given the insults that were to be hurled across the table. Alex Stepney thought the scene resembled something from a third-rate Western, which suggests The Doc to be the semi-hinged Ernest Borgnine figure who goes ape in the final reel. United-chronicler Michael Crick preferred the gangsterist image: Brando sorting out his feuding lieutenants maybe. Arthur Albiston was excused on the grounds of his youth – just as in classic butchery scenes, the women and children are evacuated beforehand. The players, emboldened by their collectivism, at least got their gripes aired. But in return, Docherty turned to every single player and lambasted him in as vicious a manner as possible, all the while swigging from a full bottle of brandy. Stepney, in his autobiography, lists only two of the Doc's comments (telling Houston and Stepney how crap they were) allegedly because none of the rest is printable. Not, it appears, on libel grounds but because of the Obscene Publications Act. The air 'cleared' – and the bottle drained – the Doc stormed off into the night.

Some will tell you none of this mattered; others that it was never the same again. Certainly, none who was there ever forgot it. And equally, the powers-that-be back home, be they 'junior board' or senior, heard all about it – hardly an exhibition of Busbyesque managerial class was it? Chance for another turn on the knife-sharpener...

Nevertheless, no-one could have expected that the blades would enter the back at the very moment of Docherty's greatest triumph, winning the 1977 FA Cup. Scarcely had the dregs from the post-Final party bottles been swigged when the corrosive truth began to leak out with mercurial effect. It transpired that the Doc, already well-established as a Falstaffian rogue of the first order, had been playing away – and it was the physio's wife who'd been coming on as sub for his missus. For a solid week, the story barely left the front pages. And for many observers, first reactions were hilarity mixed with a grudging admiration. As a roly-poly middle-aged bloke in the most pressurised of jobs, he'd done pretty well to net a good-looking woman seventeen years younger than himself and keep it quiet for so long, hadn't he? But to our dismay, the affair was transformed from tabloid comedy to tragedy. The Edwards' initial assurance that Tommy's confession was "a private matter" melted under the heat of insiders' outrage and within a week he'd been fired.

For a couple of years afterwards, many Reds on the jury of public opinion were prepared to accept much of Tommy's own defence that he'd done nothing wrong or unprofessional in merely falling for his true love. But as Docherty continued his post-United career as manager-turned-pundit, he has managed to alienate huge swathes of former supporters and demonstrate the very character facets which so enraged his 70s enemies. The court cases of '78 and '81 (of which more follows) did the initial damage; his later erratic public pronouncements, in particular during the Cantona Affair, turned many remaining Docherty boys off him for good. Re-examining the defence pleas in a rather different light produces an altogether less favourable summing-up.

If his sacking was a question of morality, then let us get one thing straight: it had nothing to do with the edicts of Catholicism but the ethics of professionalism. There never was any evidence that "Catholic directors' wives" had anything to do with this whatsoever. They were easy culprits to finger, 'meddlesome women' being a good line to sell to the Stretford Enders. True though it might have been that the 'junior board' and a director or two, particularly Denzil Haroun, were outraged, they would not in themselves have been sufficiently powerful to overthrow the Edwardses' original judgment. No, surely the key moment came when the twin guardians of the Club's honour acted – when Paddy Crerand phoned Sir Matt in Ireland, told him the score, and awaited Busby's return to OT on the first flight back. Not such easy culprits to finger, hey?

The issue, surely, was never adultery *per se*. As Docherty correctly guessed, the Edwardses would agree that this particular sin was hardly a novelty at OT and certainly not one over which they'd be prepared to get on their high horse. After all, "It's been going on since Adam and Eve" was reportedly Martin Edwards' first shoulder-shrugging reaction. Instead, as Willie Morgan said, "The thing that got him sacked wasn't the falling-in-love – it was making the physio reserve-team trainer, sending him on scouting trips and giving his wife one while he was away." Docherty was manager, Brown his colleague and subordinate; in Morgan's view, this was a professional's betrayal of trust, an abuse of position and responsibility. How could it ever just be "a personal matter?" Laurie Brown had not only suffered a disaster in his personal life but in his professional life too – in turn, the Club's honour and solidarity were at stake. How could we be Manchester *United* if such activities were in any way excused? If there was a moral point that exercised Busby, Crerand and all those who supported them, this was it. And in that judgment, they were undoubtedly correct.

As it happened, there was more to consider than simply adultery and the professional misconduct therein. Mysterious sightings of private investigators trailing Tommy had brought allegations about ticket-touting, incidents on tour, car crashes and private prosecutions for assault. Although the allegations came to naught. With Tommy's healthy list of foes, who hired the detectives was anybody's guess. Evidence of the sort collected by Willie Morgan for his libel case also reached the Board's ears. At one point during the Alderley Edge meeting at which the Board told Docherty he was sacked, Martin Edwards cited Docherty's cup final ticket scams as a contributory factor to their decision. Docherty replied that he'd been doing it since 1959, had hardly been secretive about it, and could have added that United players had done the same in the past. Maybe so: but there's surely a qualitative difference between underpaid players selling off spares in the early 60s and a manager inviting Stan Flashman into the director's lounge for large-scale trading! The barman on duty that day had the right idea – he tried to punch both of them when he saw what they were up to.

If, in brutal terms, the exchange United made of Brown for Docherty damaged our playing prospects, it did safeguard the Club's soul. That is far more important, just as style means more than success on the field. Some will scoff that such concerns are hypocritical, given the minor naughtinesses that littered United's post-war years. But arguing that because Busby's United once allowed the odd irregular payment, the men of that era had no right to condemn Docherty is just

119

facile. Dochertyites often say that July 1977 was the Busbyites last stand, their final revenge. Perhaps: but after making so many enemies and giving them so much ammunition, Docherty only had himself to blame. In any event, I would prefer to think of it as the last time the Club made a stand for morality and decency, or at least those parts of the Club's family which still believed in these Busbyesque ideals.

So forty-odd days after his greatest triumph at Wembley, the Doc's reign was over. Derby County got their man after all but Docherty never reached the heights again. Eventually in 1988 he was free to marry Mary and had already begun to carve out a new career as a media mouth. As a 'personality', he had seemed ideally suited for a club such as ours. Anyone who saw his team at its best will always retain a place in their heart for him – or rather, perhaps, just for his footballing ideals – however badly he behaves. He played on the fans' every erogenous zone – he gave us a young team, predominantly home-developed, who truly believed in attacking football, who exhibited a never-say-die attitude and played with the flair, passion and skill for which United have traditionally stood.

As a man and a character, however... A United player once said "If Tommy said 'good morning' to you, you went outside to check for rain clouds." Cynical historians say he "was perfectly suited for the Edwardses' United" – but surely not for Busby's. I suppose it all depends on how you saw the balance of the nature of the Club in the mid-to-late 70s, torn between different moralities and schools of thought. Docherty might be charitably viewed as merely a victim of that existential conflict. One should be generous, maybe, and remember him for his team's performances, not his own deficiencies – just as one shouldn't dismiss the products of Wagner and T S Eliot simply because of their disgusting personal politics. Though I admit this can be difficult when you're listening to him spout on Piccadilly Radio.

There would be a painful postscript for Tommy to endure. They do say revenge is a dish best served cold but in the case of Docherty versus his Legion of Enemies, this was surely a platter almost frozen solid. By November 1978, when the Morgan libel proceedings finally began, all the main participants had already left Old Trafford. Willie Morgan, as the recipient of the libel writ, did at least have two years to prepare his battle-plan. The result was an overwhelming arsenal of offensive weaponry which succeeded in making plaintiff Docherty look like the defendant: 29 counts of alleged impropriety and an array of celebrated star defence witnesses including Stepney, Macari, Ted MacDougall, Paddy Crerand and Denis Law. Oh, and Barry Fry was there too. Court-reporting legislation meant that every allegation could be aired and repeated in print without fear of action. Tommy now admits that "sueing Morgan was the biggest mistake of my life", a statement of the bleedin' obvious, of course. Yet when he wails he initially took superb legal advice that he had a winnable case, you wonder how smart Docherty ever was. Knowing that every man he'd ever crossed would emerge in court, that every questionable act would be disinterred for examination and that the whole caboodle would be repeated verbatim across the front pages, how did he ever hope to emerge with any credit even if he had won? For, looking back, it appears the question of the case was never "is Tommy the worst manager ever?" as Morgan had alleged. Instead, it rapidly descended into a dissection of Docherty's character, probity and wholesomeness. Anyone who's ever seen Docherty's facial language when questioned on controversial matters would have known he'd be a witness-box disaster. The intense rapid blinking, the tremble in the lips...if any observer could see this, why couldn't he or his briefs?

At the end of the third painful day, during which Docherty admitted lying to the court about the Law Affair, he withdrew the action and turned to face costs which reached nearly £60,000 plus a consequent perjury trial. If The Doc *vs.* Morgan had been catastrophic for his reputation and bank-balance, then The Doc *vs.* The Queen threatened his very liberty. But few tears were shed for him amongst the defence witnesses. Denis Law had been reluctant to enter the box – never a problem for him as a player – but Paddy Crerand was actually disappointed to miss out: "I had a thing or two to say," he grinned. Indeed he had: the Doc Treatment Paddy endured was less well-known and deserved the airing already granted to Law and Morgan's tales of woe. How Docherty appointed Crerand assistant manager and seemed to under-mine him within weeks. How he froze him out, asking Pat to leave dressing rooms before games and secretly re-organising coach departures to make sure he missed matches. And most contentiously, how Docherty told the Board Crerand was sup-posedly drinking too much to get himself organised and do the job. Docherty eventually got his wish, as he always did with black artistry – Paddy left the Club via Northampton, invaluable services lost to United for a decade.

Paddy would've been able to help out with another juicy allegation which caught the media's fancy: that Docherty sup-posedly pocketed a large bung in cash from Dunstable Town for George Best's temporary services. Crerand would have tes-tified to witnessing the cash hand-over, all of which Docherty continued to deny after the case despite Barry Fry and chair-man Cheeseman's corroborating accounts, though the issue was never to reach the courts. Add to that the rehashing of Docherty's Cup Final ticket touting, used as a partial excuse for his 1977 sacking, and the football world had a portrait of Docherty's personal and financial dealings which was hardly going to strengthen a job-hunting CV. And so Tommy would claim that the case ruined him professionally. But then, who had brought it in the first place? Nemesis had followed hubris, as always. Like Kasparov fatefully taking on Deep Thought and losing, Docherty had appeared to believe his end-game winning streak had made him invulnerable. He would escape prison in 1981 only after a court decided his courtroom lies were "not deliberate".

Since 1981, Docherty has responded in a variety of ways to these events. At times, with some justification, he has defended certain behaviour by citing precedent: everyone dealt in Cup Final tickets, he was just more honestly brazen about it. In other matters, he will continue hotly to deny what every other witness will aver is the truth. Sometimes, he simply refuses to refer to the crux of an issue; elsewhere, he has changed his tune to suit the harmony of the times. Willie Morgan told Jim White that in court, Morgan's barrister asked Willie to tug on his gown every time Doc lied in the box: after half an hour, he abandoned the tactic. So frequent was the tugging from below that the gown was losing its tailored shape.

But to be a truly effective Machiavellian requires so much more cunning, intelligence and thoroughness than Tommy ever possessed. Lies must go undetected, back-stabbings left without dabs, bungs passed without witnesses, bad-mouthing confined to the most trusted. The truly evil black art practitioners can meet all these requirements. Tommy was never evil; he was just a bit of a bad lad burdened with a credibility gap. But he hurt people and did them harm nonetheless – I guess that is what he still had to pay for in the end.

THE
BUTCHERS

You have to tread carefully before you suggest Louis Edwards was a villain. Even though he's dead and can't sue, too many at Old Trafford still think kindly of the old bounder to make Louis-bating an entirely safe occupation. Michael Crick, who wrote the outstanding United book of the 80s *Betrayal of a Legend* exposing the Edwards family entrails, was surprised to find that his season-ticket wasn't immediately cancelled upon publication. But he knows it's unlikely he'll find a receptive ear at the ground should he ever need a favour. Even Eamon Dunphy, who slaughtered a few sacred cows in his epic *A Strange Kind Of Glory*, demurred at fingering Louis for cuffs, suggesting he was just a good-time "Billy" with unorthodox methods. And there's the unanswerable point that Old Trafford Stadium as we know it today was largely Louis's vision, at least until refined by the Knighton blueprint in '89. Mind you, plenty will argue that begatting Martin and foisting him upon the club was sin enough; and even Dunphy has to accept that "Sir Matt's lapdog" did rather turn on his owner and dump in his lap. One observation remains, I think, unchallengable: that MUFC plc as we know it, and often loathe it, today was an almost inevitable consequence of actions inspired by Louis. Of course, no-one knows whether he'd approve of 1998's MUFC if he came back to haunt the place today but he'd certainly recognise its parentage. The plc, and all that goes with it, is his bastard son.

Of course it's hugely ironic that it was Matt Busby in 1958 who got Louis onto the Board in the first place – as full of wry hindsight as, say, Law and Morgan vouching for Tommy Doc to the Board in 1972. Even after 1962, when Louis began working almost full-time to extend his power within the Club, Matt could still look upon Louis as an ally doing his best to shore up the Busby position. For Louis always backed Matt, no matter what: that was his function, and he knew it. So, for example, when United realised they'd need to break the transfer record to get Denis Law, there was no problem – Louis twisted enough arms to ensure Matt got his man. Louis, so the conventional wisdom had it, was just a good-time guy, happy to bask in the glory Busby reflected all around the Club's upper echelons, delighted to be able to gladhand the stars and hand out the cigars 'n' champers. Coming from the dodgy end of a dodgy industry (low-grade meat products), Louis had already done very well for himself. But behind the *bonhomie* lurked a sharp operator, intent on grasping control of the Club. He had dodgy figures like corrupt ex-councillor Frank Farrington knocking on doors around town every night, buying up every available United share from gullible punters; when the Board nervously voted to stop principals' share-balances being altered, he simply got his brother-in-law to do some buying on the family's behalf instead. Like Atlantic waters creeping through Titanic bulkheads, by the end of '63 the Edwardses' share of the club was beginning to increase in size geometrically, tilting the Club towards Louis's slavering embrace. By the time chairman Harold Hardman died in 1965, there was only one possible successor: Louis Edwards was elected unopposed. He effectively owned the Club anyway and had secured it for an outlay of only £35,000. The Board's individuals had been too weak to stop him even if they'd wanted to; only Hardman himself had vehemently opposed Louis's ascent, and his death thus removed the final obstacle. The *coup d'état* complete, Louis wisely sat back, continuing to make his money from the Edwards family meat business whilst treating the football club as his prestige showcase like so many businessmen-cum-chairmen before him. It would be over a decade before Phase Two would come into operation – the conversion of Manchester United from rich man's plaything to cash-cow. Meanwhile, as long as Old Trafford Stadium was being modernised and funds continued to be made available for incoming transfers, few bothered to examine too closely the financial affairs of Louis Edwardses' United. Isolated outbreaks of irregularity, such as United's 1969 fine for making illegal payments to players, were easily brushed under the carpet. Even relegation brought no censure of Louis's financial dealings: after the spending spree Docherty had embarked upon in '73, no-one could claim Louis hadn't made the backing available to the management. Instead it would be the Edwardses' family business that began to stink, which would in turn infect the good name of United and eventually put us on the road to becoming a plc.

Few realised that by the mid-70s the Edwards family firm was in trouble. When the Edwards clan bailed out in 1978, it only cost tycoon James Gulliver £100,000 to take control and the firm's true worth stood at a mere half-million. (Ironically, Gulliver transformed the outfit into Argyll Foods and made it a £2 billion outfit by the mid-80s, which might illustrate the gulf in financial acumen between him and the Edwardses – perhaps precisely that between an acknowledged genius and guys with no A-levels.) If the Edwards family wanted to make serious money, it would now have to be through United alone. They would begin with a rights issue.

Nevertheless, it was always argued that the primary purpose of the issue was to raise cash for the manager to spend – £1 million, to be exact. But it wasn't just the cynics who saw through such protestations. Both Sir Matt and Les Olive opposed the issue, correctly pointing out that United's cash reserves, supporter-base and healthy Development Association accounts were ample reservoirs should further transfer funds be required. And when rebel activist John Fletcher proposed a less unusual scheme which would've raised £2 million, the Board oddly argued that such a sum was more than required.

An indication of the greater motivation was provided by Louis Edwards in 1977 when, according to Michael Crick, he asked a colleague, "How much do you think a United fan would pay to have a share certificate on his wall?" He and his advisers had been considering a 'free share' issue, giving, say, ten new free shares for each one already held. Big shareholders could then sell off thousands to sentimental loyal fans without seriously threatening their own control of the club. It wouldn't just have been a licence to print share certificates but a licence to print money. Fortunately, FA rules were discovered to prohibit such a scheme.

The rights issue as finally constituted was the next best

thing. For every share already held, each holder could buy 208 new ones at £1 each. As the figure of £1 was an undervaluation, holders could then sell off as much as they liked at a good profit. Sure, you had to find the money to buy your allotted allocation first – but when you know you're bound to cash in later, you lay such a risk-free bet without hesitation. As far as the Edwardses were concerned, there was only one problem. They only held just under half the shares as of 1977. Since keeping control of the Club was almost as important as making money, they would need a much greater holding to maximise the benefits of the scheme, and to ensure it would be passed in the first place. Ideally, they'd want to acquire enough shares – say, three-quarters – so they could sell off a huge pile, make a mint, yet still retain 50+ per cent control. And at one point, there was talk that these £1 shares might eventually hit £8 each; the potential profits were enormous.

It would be a mighty fine trick to pull off, to increase control and make a fortune without any fundamental change in the underlying business; indeed, a rare near-impossibility. For how could they hope to acquire more shares cheaply enough before the issue? Surely everyone else would be seeing pound signs before the eyes too? Er, not if they didn't know what was planned. Beryl Norman and Elizabeth Hardman, neither of whom were privy to the issue project, were both persuaded to sell their small stakes to the Edwardses (in one case with the transaction being partially made with a bundle of readies to avoid tax). Director Alan Gibson parted with a huge stake of nearly a quarter of the club's shares only after being told the rights issue had been dropped.

The Edwardses now had 74 per cent of the shares and could proceed to drive through the rights issue plan before capitalising on the aftermath. But they gained them only by breaking the Club's own articles, which stated shares had to be offered for sale to the Board as a whole first. Far more seriously, the crucial holdings had been acquired through, essentially, insider trading. In 1977/78, this was not illegal, merely massively unethical: the law was changed to make it a crime in the 80s when the Government realised there were fewer and fewer proper gentlemen in the City. Before Thatcherism perverted the nation, insider dealing was simply seen as a sin, as something no self-respecting man of honour would stoop to – for in order to benefit from an insider's prescience, some poor genuine investor outside the loop had to get stiffed. That is what happened to the women and Gibson. If the women, for example, who received £22,000 for their holdings had held on to them and instead invested £25,000 to take up their rights issue allocation, they would now be worth about £6 million. Gibson's stake, sold for £200,000, would if maintained now command well over £50 million for his surviving family. The sordid claims of notorious 80s white-collar criminals that insider trading should be classed as a "victimless crime" look rather hollow in such a light, don't they?

Once the warfare had ceased and the issue passed, many were prepared to rally around the Establishment flag where it felt comfortable and warm. David Meek, naturally, predicted we would soon be applauding the deal, and that Louis had a good record of stewardship and could be trusted. As he spoke, Granada's *World in Action* had already begun their year-long investigation into Louis Edwards, their interest ironically sparked by the very rights issue which was supposed to have saved his career. When Granada broadcast "The Man Who Bought United" in early 1980, it created the greatest media furore since Docherty's sacking.

United were already at a low enough ebb in January 1980

without needing another kicking from Granada TV: out of the Cup, humiliated by Liverpool a few weeks back and our big new transfer sensation was Nickolai 'Zombie' Jovanovic. But on the night of 28 January *World in Action* let loose what might have been the most damaging broadside yet. In a meticulously researched, devastatingly venomous half-hour programme, they ruined a reputation built up over three decades in business.

First, they retold the rather grubby story of how Louis came to take over United, from the sly 60s manipulations to the outright immorality of the rights issue. (The secret phone recording in which Edwards airily dismissed capital gains tax offences as mere "technicalities" was hardly going to endear him to watching Revenue inspectors.) Then they turned to his meat business, forcefully demonstrating with eyewitness evidence that his empire sold their low-grade meat via a network of bribery, corruption and dodgy accounting. It was a nice touch to note that much of his produce had ended up being eaten by our local kids in their school dinners; suddenly good ol' Uncle Louis looked more like the fiddling uncle in *Tommy*. And finally, there was his conduct of business at United – a secret slush fund was revealed, from which payments would be made illegally to parents as inducements to get their sons to sign for United. The fund had allegedly been built up using non-existent expenses and other false accounting devices. The overall impression of the Club left with the viewer was of a particularly shabby used-car dealership, run by an unlovable variant on the Arthur Daley model, not of a world-famous sporting institution. Louis, conveniently, died within weeks of a heart attack in his bath at home.

Before his death he had turned for advice to such luminaries as QC George Carman (who'd got Jeremy Thorpe acquitted of conspiracy to commit murder) and Lord Goodman, Harold Wilson's notorious and fearsome legal enforcer, but the telling consequence of their advice was that United and Edwards took no action. The allegations stood, unchallenged. Indeed, Granada had stacks' more information, witnesses and allegations for deployment if necessary: as one insider put it, thirty minutes was never going to be enough to summarise thirty years of misbehaviour.

Within 24 hours, seven local MPs – a class of public figure who usually go out of their way to back MUFC lest they lose their freebies – had called for a government probe. The FA announced an inquiry into claims of false accounting and irregular share dealings. The Department of Trade and the Football League began looking into allegations about bribing schoolboy players' parents. And finally the scariest buggers of all, the Inland Revenue, began gearing up to crawl all over the Edwards empire's records. Even the police wanted to see videos of the programme, just in case anybody had missed a stray indictable allegation or two. Had God himself appeared in the centre circle to bellow, "Oi, Louis, I want a word with you," few would've been surprised.

That Louis personally was in major shit was obvious to all. Many Reds were content to abandon him to his fate, although others were prepared to argue that he'd acted for the greater good of the club. For example, everybody bribed kids' parents to get schoolboy talent – so what if United were just better at it than most, and had been unfortunate enough to get caught? And many in the press followed the *Mirror* line that a general investigation was overdue: "Libel laws have so far prevented a football Watergate. But corruption in the game extends to the highest levels. If this programme opens the way for a full inquiry, then soccer will benefit." But what concerned

United fans above all were the possible sanctions that might have been applied to the Club as a whole. As one extravagant headline put it: "United Might Win The Title – But Be Expelled From The League!" Only the fact that no individual United player had wittingly benefitted directly from Edwards' corruption could be put forward in mitigation against the team being made to suffer. And as the farce over United's European 'ban' had proved two years earlier when the Club had to fight to overturn disqualification after crowd trouble in St Etienne, there was no guarantee that the authorities would let such niceties stand in their way. When United met Bristol City after the broadcast, banners proclaiming "Edwards Out!" were clearly visible, and hostile chants sufficiently audible for even such notorious cloth-ears as the United board.

Attention hazily focussed on son Martin, a virtually silent director since 1970, who suddenly became a potential player at the top should Louis fall on his sword. Or slip in his bath. All we knew about Martin was that he was some kind of accountant, spent most of his 70s Saturdays at his rugby club rather than Old Trafford and, according to one profile which dug up his O-level records, was a bit of a minor prep school mediocrity. Some wondered whether this was a case of better the red devil you know.

Looking back, one could argue that such sordidness seems so very tame and even inconsequential. The shenanigans with his dodgy pies never mattered: to find one company who dealt honestly with 60s and 70s councils would be a miracle. Compared to the Poulson scandal, this was very small beer, or sausage-rolls, indeed. Moreover now we know every club does, and always did, use under-the-counter methods in dealing with both the Revenue and stars of the future. Secretly, many might approve: if the end result is more money and suc-

135

cess for United, who cares? Were we really so naive then?

Perhaps not: maybe it was just the shock, coming so soon after the Docherty affair, of having Sir Matt's own club, supposed paragons of virtue, exposed as being less than saintly in such a blockbusting fashion. Some thought it also exposed a hypocrisy, the Chairman who'd fired a man for alleged dishonesty and infidelity revealed to be a bit of a crook himself. Louis's brown-bag tinkering and minor fiddling could perhaps be put down to well-intended roguishness. But insider dealing and breaking promises to Sir Matt was another.

Funnily enough, the £1 million proceeds from the rights issue never appeared to be spent as such. Wilkins's purchase was easily offset by the summer sales of Pancho, Greenhoff and McCreery. The new goalkeeper Martin Edwards had suggested financing did materialise in the form of Gary Bailey, but at a cost of five, not five hundred, thousand. Nor, admittedly, did the share price rocket quite as much as the Edwardses had hoped. Martin sold some immediately to repay a third of the loan he'd taken out but chose to keep the rest. Publicly, he became a martyr to his overdraft, often pulling out the violins in later years to describe how he'd had to struggle along with his debt. But in fact, he was soon sitting on a realisable profit of millions, not to mention his shareholding in other companies; the overdraft was maintained out of choice, not absolute necessity. Within just five years of the issue, his stake had sensationally exploded in value to £10 million. Only then did the ironies become apparent, as Edwards twice in the 80s came within inches of cashing in and selling out. For back in '78, those arguing for general flotation had been beaten down by protestations that the Edwardses must maintain their control, allowing them to continue to nurture the club without having to fend off predators. Those hoodwinked into selling their shares to the Edwardses were fed the same line: we're just trying to ensure our control. But when Knighton and Maxwell came a-calling in the 80s, it would be a rather different story, as we'll recall in the next chapter.

By then of course, Martin was Club chairman, succeeding father Louis virtually upon his death in March 1980. Many Reds and non-Reds alike were disappointed that the game's most loved and respected figure, Sir Matt Busby, had not been appointed at least interim chairman. But the largely unknown and untested Martin seized the vacant slot. Edwards, rather inelegantly, appeared to blame Sir Matt for Louis's death, remarking in 1990 that had Matt backed the rights issue from the start, no controversy would have arisen and no *World in Action* investigation instigated. That's some combination of sophistry and insensitivity in just one sentence. Sir Matt, of course, had objectively been correct to oppose the deal in any event. But Louis had hardly helped himself keep Matt onside. The gents' agreement which the two had that Matt would eventually be chairman was seemingly never going to come to pass, as Matt had begun to realise. However, when Louis went back on a solemn promise to elevate Sandy Busby to the Board and instead promoted the claims of his own kid Roger, he had forfeited any right to expect Matt's support. Somehow, that breach of promise seems to me to be more regrettable than most of what *World in Action* alleged. Like father, like son: so it should have been no surprise when Martin eagerly clambered upon the platform his father had built for him to beat Sir Matt to the vacant chairmanship in 1980. Matt didn't want to fight, and so accepted the Presidency with typical grace, a grace some felt Martin hadn't deserved and which he himself failed to match. It is said Matt was only looking for a couple of years at the top to complete a career in the best possible way but Martin wasn't offering.

The result of 1978's shadiness? Well, Martin Edwards has pulled in hundreds of thousands of pounds in salaries and bonuses, millions in sales of share parcels and seen his £600,000 holding grow to £60 million. Perhaps to take issue with that is to succumb to personal jealousy and class envy. We have, after all, just won four Championships: there's not much time left for quibbling about remuneration when you're celebrating glorious trophies all the time. But we're heading into uncertain times as a Club. Les Olive's warnings in a letter sent to Louis in 1978 come to mind: that the rights issue paved the way to excessive dividend payments – and by implication a slavery to market sentiment – and to the threat that the Club might one day fall into unwelcome hands as a result of the opening up of United's shares to a wider dealership. United paid out £14 million in dividends alone between 1992 and 1997, during a period when our net balance of transfer expenditure had only amounted to a few million. Predators circle the Club, both friendly and hostile, threatening to take us God knows where. The share price and earnings-per-share ratio have become as important as our League position: never forget former Finance Director Robin Launders' suggestion that a Club now need not be winning trophies to maximise market potential. I could go on with a full-scale rant about the deficiencies of United's modern plc status but you'll have heard it all before.

* * *

We could also, of course, devote a whole Red Devil chapter simply to Edwards as chairman, taking on every 'political' issue of the last 18 years, with most of which my class of 'activist supporter' would find fault – but you can find plenty of that elsewhere and it would fill a book in itself. Technically, Edwards has been remarkably well-behaved anyway, with only the odd minor breach of regulations such as paying the agent Denis Roach for Mark Hughes's sale in '86, breaching FA Cup ticket regulations in '83 or allowing Revenue contraventions later in the decade. Naturally, there are plenty of unproven allegations knocking about but no libel lawyer would let us print them; in any event, as far as most hardcore fans are concerned, even if these were to surface they would fade into insignificance when set against the real *casus belli* – his overall, plc-worshipping, *Brave New World* policy agenda. Encouraging, and kow-towing to, the new breed of bourgeois fan; ignoring the traditional supporter; squeezing resources for wages and fees in favour of shareholder enrichment…this is the stuff that makes Martin a Devil in many eyes.

There is an impressionistic irony here. Louis was the "crook", the dodgy dealer, the midwife to all this at its rather hole-in-the-corner birth. Martin benefitted and is now shiny and clean, a paradigm of good behaviour and fiscal rectitude: his office will never see a brown paper bag or bundle of well-thumbed readies. Yet the tackiness of the modern United, with its consultancy fees, share options, executive incentive schemes and directors' service agreements – the paraphernalia of the 90s fat-cat corporate trough – somehow seems more unsavoury than any of Louis's antics. There was an earthy honesty about Louis's dishonesty, if you see what I mean: today, the fact that grotesque self-enrichment is so antiseptically legitimised, then rubbed in our faces via gushing media tributes and glossy Accounts brochures, pains me. Especially when you remember how some of these people got into these positions in the first place...

So much for the public face of Martin Edwards: oily smooth, well-pampered. Privately, a rather more appealing, raffish character emerges; from time to time you catch sight of it on the front pages of the tabloids, usually in a Cup Final week. (As guaranteed as the rising sun is that in the run-up to any big United event, prominent Reds will get steamy calls from several panting hacks asking for info on the latest alleged peccadilloes of club management. Said stories get front page splashes on Cup Final days, presumably in an effort to undermine morale. I can't speak for the players, but it tends to have precisely the opposite effect on the fans.) Martin is often the target for such investigations, though on largely dubious grounds: apparently, because he was on the Board at the time of Docherty's sacking for immoral conduct, that makes him fair game for 'public interest' stories about his private life on the charge of hypocrisy. Disgracefully disingenuous, of course, especially given that he himself never wanted the Doc sacked, but the results remain hugely entertaining.

I hasten to add that I wouldn't allege any of the stories are true but one can't help noticing he's never actually sued for libel. Still, there might be an innocent explanation for that. A good friend of mine knew Martin better than most for much of the past decade and I asked him why Martin never took anyone to court, no matter what muck they threw at him – after all, the UK's draconian defamation laws are grotesquely skewed towards the plaintiff. His answer was that Martin valued his privacy too much and that his shyness inhibited him from putting himself forward as a court-room witness. Nobody ever comes out of a libel trial with an enhanced reputation, whether they win or lose, and no-one can control what comes out in court and is then gleefully reported verbatim under the laws of privilege. Best to ignore the two-day tabloid wonder and then get on with your life, my friend observed.

So even when the story was outrageously unjust, Martin would still prefer to keep schtum. Especially as his job was never at risk at any time: he was hardly going to sack himself for allegedly being a bad lad, was he? An example was provided of a story which had alleged Martin had been visiting a private Cheshire address for afternoon pleasures. The truth was that it had been a case of mistaken identity – the 'culprit' resembled Martin from a distance. And as the chap in question was someone close to Martin, he chose to let the story wither rather than risk exposing the bloke in question by 'selfishly' proving his own innocence. That reflects rather well on old Martin, doesn't it? The old school code of conduct in operation, perhaps: don't squeal, don't grass and don't complain.

Those stories that have emerged, particularly three which made tabloid front pages in 1990 and 1994, certainly surprised those fans who had pigeon-holed Martin as a strait-laced Cheshire stiff, more concerned with balance-sheets than satin ones. His public demeanour – diffident, guarded, faltering, cold – didn't seem to be that of the Lothario the tabloids were portraying him as. 'Good ol' Louis' would've been a different matter; you could imagine a champers-swilling, cigar-chomping high-life "Billy" getting up to a bit of how's-yer-father. But Martin, with all the charisma of the small-town accountant that he essentially is? Surely not. Yet watch Martin at a social function, and a groovier picture emerges. The fact is that women seem incredibly attracted to him. He doesn't prowl around on the pull – not that he would want to, Mr

Lawyer – because he doesn't need to: the babes flock to him. At the opening of the Red Cafe, for example, the assorted B-list celebs and C-list bimbettes weren't circling the players but were instead hovering nervously near Martin's table, eager to catch the head honcho's eye. Alright, so there might be a touch of the Mrs Merton Question here – "So what first attracted you to the millionaire Martin Edwards?" – but then again, he was in a room full of millionaires. No, the fact is that a lot of women fancy his boyish looks and easy charm. And charming he is: talk to anyone who's met him 'off-duty' when he's properly relaxed and they'll tell you he's urbane, polished and dryly funny. He's also in good physical shape; now you can add the £60 million to that package and appreciate that the babe-magnet factor is high.

Sadly, even as discerning a chap as Martin can't help attracting the rather distasteful kind of female attention highlighted by the *People* in April 1990. "SEX, CASH AND BLACK-MAIL SENSATION!" screamed the front page, as it reported that a 26-year-old alleged ex-mistress had asked for £100,000 from Martin to buy a flat for herself. Said flat was not, unfortunately, earmarked to be a convenient cozy venue for further rumpy-pumpy but, as a letter sent by her to Edwards implied, a consideration in exchange for her good work in keeping the affair silent in the face of press queries. Oops: some might call that blackmail, m'lud. As indeed did Martin, whom the paper claimed had gone straight to lawyer 'Mo-Mo' Watkins with the missive. Caroline Wyke, a rather fit, leggy brunette with charming globes, had acknowledged in the letter that "our affair is finished" but regrettably hadn't gone into much gory detail. Fortunately, undercover *People* reporters traced her to the perfume counters at Hoopers, a notorious hotspot for those seeking scrummy Cheshire scorchers at work in high heels and black tights. Over dinner, the tabloid sleaze-monger revelled in the details provided by the unwitting lady. "I found him charming and kind. I spent a couple of nights in hotels with him...he was petrified of being recognised." (See, he's such a shy, self-effacing boy.) "He said he had had other affairs, one of which lasted a long time. We talked a lot about his wife but I didn't really want to know." A-ha – perhaps it was all a novel form of marriage guidance counselling?

Denials all round soon followed, although the *People* claimed to have everything on tape which, had 0891 numbers been around, we could all have enjoyed. And no-one sued either. By far the most amusing instant reaction was Tommy Docherty's, who blasted "Edwards must go" in the next morning's *Express* and dropped such pearlers as "he should have been more conscious of United's image" and "he has been far too indiscreet for a national football institution." In any scandalous situation, you always know that if your main critic is Docherty, you've nothing to worry about; Edwards' family all publicly backed their man, and with a Wembley place secured that very weekend, United settled back to watch it all blow over.

Well, at least until the following Sunday anyway. Back came the *People* with the best Edwards story yet, all over the front and inside pages: "SOCCER BOSS AND THE TV NEWSREADER: He put their night of love on expenses." Now we realised that the *People's* blackmail story the previous week had merely been the journalistic equivalent of an aim-setting early free kick – this was now the full Beckham-curl Monty. For starters, not only did we punters know who the woman was, we saw her virtually every week on the telly: come on down Lynette Lithgow, handsome petite BBC newshound whose Trinidadian lilt had tickled many a male fancy.

Moreover, the affair was alleged to be a long-termer, rather than the all-too-forgiveable quick legover with an available ex-model. Better still, there were pictures: not quite *in flagrante*, unfortunately, but certainly on the way to a bit of *delicto*, with one snap showing the alleged lovers' lips just a lust-charged centimetre apart. The *People* even had a series of receipts, full of exquisite detail. The couple had spent £70 at Langan's Brasserie, famous for its celeb diners but also regarded as just a little bit *déclassé*/flash Harry. They'd checked themselves into the £500 suite at the Royal Lancaster Hotel under the names Mr and Mrs Edwards – how the real 'Er Indoors must've loved reading that on Sunday morning. And Martin had charged the entire jaunt to MUFC expenses, on the basis that he was on Club duty, taking in the Chelsea fixture that week-end. Doubtless that is why the receipts showed they didn't order room service breakfast until after 11 am next morning – a hard-working night of Club business must have seen the midnight oil being burned. (Or should that be "smeared"?)

Still, nice to see that Martin was allegedly considerate enough to remember to visit the lady on Valentine's Day at her Bowden flat, where one hopes he gave her more than chocolates; credit too for his admirable lack of racial prejudice. It has always been a stereotype held dear by we great unwashed that the directorial class are likely to be your arche-typal gin-swilling golf-club blazered-racist breed, so Martin's alleged 10-month fling with a black girl rather holed that theory.

Despite the expenses malarkey, a section of Red laddery could only admire the chairman for his playing performance – two megababes, possibly being run at the same time. *Red Issue* immediately rechristened its letters page as "Ups and Downs With Lynette" in tribute and printed several excellently lurid cartoons featuring the chairman and newsreader 'on club business'. They made the most of it, because surely such a scandal could never recur; six tabloid pages in one week had to be enough to make the chairman tighten up his PR control, right?

Wrong. *Red Issue* had the type-resetters in again four years later as the letters page became "Debbie's Dribblings" in honour of 28-year-old blonde Debbie Miller. The timing, naturally, was everything: United were due to play in the Coca-Cola Cup Final that afternoon, as the *News Of The World* filled page one with "MY SEX GAMES WITH UNITED BOSS" and a full-length pic of Debbie in her United kit. Note the step up in sleaze value to the *Screws* rather than the *People*, a guarantee that juicy detail lies within. And, once again, Martin's lad-value increased, for Miss Miller was quite a looker in a Gennifer Flowers kind of way (thank God United don't have interns, hey?) with a large beaming mouth which she put to use, claiming to have given Martin a "Gillian Taylforth" in his BMW when no convenient hotel was at hand.

Once inside various provincial hotels, according to Debbie, Martin continued to be as gentlemanly as ever. "He was very meticulous; he hung up his suit and laid his watch on his handkerchief by the bed...we made love, and later woke twice more for sex but he was always gentle. He's a wonderful lover but very straight, nothing kinky and he just likes the missionary position. In fact I wanted him to be a little rougher but he was always gentle and considerate...it's not in his nature to be selfish in bed." (Blimey, wish he was that selfless with his bonuses and salary.)

Debbie proudly declared that she'd been given a £2,000 22-carat brooch (clearly good going for a receptionist who did

145

the odd bit of promo work for pin money), and that she loved Martin; not surprisingly, she wasn't too thrilled towards the end of the relationship when Martin supposedly gave her £100 for her birthday and simply told her to "get herself something nice". Now you'd think his upbringing would've told him that's a no-no, wouldn't you? Still, she had fond memories of dressing up in various top-notch lingerie to get his motor revving and of the night they tried to shag in the car but got trapped in their own discarded clothing. And United fans were pleased to read how "we made love before watching Blackburn on TV; Martin said he hated Kenny Dalglish." And Martin's response to this latest disaster? To blanch briefly, before intoning, "I do know Debbie. But I never talk about my private life." Which made him the only person in Britain that morning not talking about it.

Since then, it's been all quiet on the Edwards front; if it's true that he never gave up the family tradition of doing naughty things with pork products, then he's found a way to keep it discreet. Reds coming back from European away trips will tell you interesting things about the alleged itineraries of some United officials, especially in places like Amsterdam, but we'll leave that to your imagination. The cumulative effect of Edwards's personal scandals on Red opinion is a strange one; there's disgust and disapproval from some, but also grudging admiration and sniggering amusement from others. One important side-effect on club policy has been the liberal attitude United take to personal conduct. Had Docherty's exposure occurred in 1997 instead of '77, for example, there's little doubt that he'd have survived. You rarely, if ever, hear Martin or his acolytes banging on about "moral values" or the "Club's good name" in relation to the occasional misbehaviour of its stars and employees, although I suppose you could argue that "Man Utd" has become so irredeemably associated with tatty naffness over the last few years that nothing could diminish the reputation anyhow. But it's nonetheless a good by-product, this willingness to disassociate public and private conduct, for it has allowed us to retain the services of such luminaries as Eric, Keano, Giggs, etc. when they've been at the centre of tabloid firestorms. In a way, we all owe a debt to the Carolines, Lynettes, Debbies for their roles in creating this attitude. Not to mention for the laughs they gave us...

THE
COUNTERFEIT
WINGER

If Willie Morgan was a poor man's George Best, what does that make Mickey Thomas? A destitute's Gordon Hill? That would be an insult to the homeless, I suppose. They've been trying to make a 70s character out of Mickey recently *à la* Stan Bowles or Alan Hudson; the carpet-baggers at *Goal* magazine even produced a book about him, slim pickings eked out over 145 threadbare pages. One might concede that he's had an interesting life, if one that has mainly consisted of low-rent, tacky sordidness and fourth-class football teams, but unlike many devils in this book, Mickey Thomas was simply never someone you aspired to emulate. No-one so lacking in the glory game's finer graces could ever be much of a role model to impressionable young fans.

They worshipped him in Wrexham, admittedly, but at Old Trafford there would only be disdain flecked with dashes of hatred. The latter came courtesy of the Gordon Hill fan club, of which I was a member, and was a touch unfair on the lad. After all, Mickey hadn't sold Gordon, had he? And there'd been a decent mourning interval inbetween Hill's tear-stained departure for Derby and Mickey's arrival. Mickey was to suffer mainly as a cipher: for to us, he was the personification of the evil Sexton regime. You could almost see Sexton pulling the strings behind his little marionette, yanking him back into midfield for tracking duties, making him run around beserkly like brainless poultry, 'doubling up' and 'tucking in' to fulfil the loathsome coaching prescriptions of the day. The comparison with Hill, a free-scoring uncontrollable lightning spirit, was painful. Gordon represented all that was good about the Docherty era – Thomas was a harbinger of its legacy's eradication.

To many in the Stretford End, it was no accident that the most boring football in United's modern history was played between November 1978 and the summer of 1981 – the exact duration of Thomas's wide-left tenancy. The wretched Welshman arrived just in time to be associated with some of our worst days, such as the triple whammy suffered at the hands of Bolton, West Brom and Liverpool that 1978 Christmas, or the awful "Midget Line" matches the following autumn when teams took it in turn to flatten our puny forward line of Coppell, Macari and Thomas. He also managed to get himself injured twice within his first year which, though hardly his fault, simply made him look even more inadequate in the big boys' league. In fact, many Reds never got over the fact that he was a lower division player at heart – yet an expensive one too – of a class we were supposed to have risen above; Docherty bought well in the lower reaches but that was when United were on the deck. Now that we were supposed to be fully rehabilitated as a major player, fishing around in Welsh pools seemed like slumming it. And Mickey was a small town lad in essence, not a big city man: throughout his career, when the world closed in on him, his first instinct would be to hare back to Colwyn Bay and hide out with his mum. Like some twitchy extra in the *Great Escape*, you always felt he was going to make a run for it, only to be impaled upon the barbed wire.

Old Trafford was no place for such a character. The likes of Macari, Jordan and McQueen were proper tough guys, mentally and physically, to whom the idea of weak-kneed escape was anathema. The United dressing room was built for big egos, cutting humour and vicious politicking, not as a nursery for small-time bags of nerves. And boy, was Mickey nervous, often on the edge of chucking up, unable to sleep before major games, forever eyeing the route back to Wales. The likes of Lou Macari (the Pisstaker-General at OT) didn't make life any easier for him, as Thomas became the favoured butt of practical jokes and sly wisecracks; contemporaries report sights of Thomas fleeing in panic whenever Lou was up for a jape, hiding wherever he could. Gradually, the demon drink began to weave its black magic, providing Mickey with a mental if not physical escape from the pressures of being a United star – and there was his new marriage to Debbie, offering home-based succour and support. A few drinking sessions and some regular TLC might have done the trick in settling Thomas down. Instead, booze and the missus caused him nothing but trouble for the rest of his time at United.

Nor did the public utterances of both Thomas and Sexton help his cause much with terrace opinion. Thomas admitted that his crossing needed work, and later remarked, "I don't attack much – I tend to drop back to help out. But I'm not a very good passer of the ball." To which most Reds would reply, "Well, what exactly are you good at, then?" Dave Sexton had replaced Hill with someone who apparently couldn't score, pass, cross or attack – but he "always gave 110 per cent and covered every blade of grass", the dread defence of workmanship that every Red hates to hear. Sexton only made matters worse: "He's come here hungry to prove himself...he won't be overawed," he boasted early on, when it was immediately evident that the chump was completely overawed. Months later, as spring arrived to find United in mid-table mediocrity, Sexton was still claiming, "Mickey's purchase has been my most important decision," as Thomas flailed about half-fit, woefully failing to either create or score a goal. Another groan-inducing Thomas quote seemed to sum up what was wrong: "There are occasions when the other players make me feel inferior with the things they can do...at Wrexham I was the star but here I come well down the list. The crowd don't come to watch me...my job is to work and run for others." Self-deprecatingly honest Mickey may have been, but this was not what Reds wanted to hear from their nominal wingers, brought up as they were on Hill, Morgan and Best.

"Honest" Mickey lost even that worthy prefix in October 1979. Already vilified by Reds for representing an alien Sextonian style and mentality, he then managed to make himself a national target too, fingered by Jimmy Hill on TV as the embodiment of something else hateful in the sport – gamesmanship. We were playing Ipswich in a top of the table clash, the country's eyes fixed on us via *Match of the Day* as we fought for the right to be Liverpool's main challengers. Mickey and an Ipswich defender were going for what appeared to be a 50/50 ball – suddenly Thomas was on the floor in the penalty box. Grimes converted what proved to be a winning spot-kick and, despite later thrashing us 6-0, Ipswich never quite managed to rejoin us in that season's title race. So far so good, except that at the very moment Thomas was on the floor listening to the ref's whistle blow for the penalty, his face was caught in close-up by the TV cameras smirking and – damningly – winking. Hill, and the legions of pundits who trampled in his wake, had no doubts as to what this signified: he'd dived and conned a potentially season-defining penalty and hadn't even the grace to hide it. Cue a tabloid three-day wonder, which unfortunately for Thomas was crystallised in time by the BBC's decision to use the Thomas close-up in its *MOTD* title sequence for what seemed like the next 50 years. Suddenly poor Mickey found himself lumped in with the old Leeds vermin as an example of everything that was rotten about the professionally-fouling, cheating, cynical 70s. Only the fact that he was too weak to be a dirty player as well prevented him from being placed above Giles and Hunter in the decade's villainy parade. It was grossly unfair but that was Mickey's trademark *modus operandi* all over; he seemingly always got caught, whatever he did in life.

So it was no surprise when he caused himself and United further unwelcome publicity when he began having marital problems. Most United players, bearing in mind the temptations laid before them, have had their strife behind bedroom doors but most of the time it rarely amounts to anything publicly. Mickey, typically, had chosen a young bride who was made for tabloid attention. As a former 'glamour model', there were plenty of juicy shots of her knocking around for which the press would always be gagging to have an excuse to use, and her sometimes excitable behaviour made for great copy in itself anyway. A trial separation was being successfully hushed up when Mickey, with his usual woeful timing, managed to drive his Rover off the road into a large hedge.

The press started sniffing about once more as a result and consequently dug up the tale of how Debbie had turfed Mickey out of their home – chucking his stuff, including a VCR, out onto the lawn, before proceeding to kick in a glass door with her bare feet, requiring twelve emergency stitches. Later, the couple would try to repair the damage by doing a 'good news' feature for the *Sunday Mirror*, in which they talked about the difficult birth of their son and the pressures of fame. Unfortunately, this tended to make many Reds even more convinced that this guy was cursed with bad luck and best dumped at the earliest opportunity. A car crash, a near-death birth, a mega-fight with the wife and a burglary, all in the space of a few weeks? In a superstitious game, this was not encouraging form.

In all his time at Old Trafford, only one shaft of light stands out from the gloom, as inexplicable as it was unexpected. As Alex Ferguson would say, we were in a Devon Loch scenario, several furlongs behind leaders Liverpool in the 1980 title race. Unbelievably, by the end of March, it would be the unlikely figure of Mickey Thomas who'd come galloping to the rescue. He'd been out for six games, treating his injury under an assortment of UV and heat lamps which appeared to effect his genetic make-up – how else to explain his roaring form when he returned, banging home four goals in five games and creating most of the others? Perhaps this was what Clayton Blackmore was up to all those years on his sun-bed, looking to replicate the Thomas Effect upon his own Welsh mediocrity? Mickey's comeback goal beat City in the worst derby of modern times, rather pleasingly deflected off Tony Henry whose goal had slanted that awful November match in City's favour. He and Jordan combined to win at Palace, whilst Liverpool lost across the capital at Spurs. Suddenly, we were game on, just four points behind with the crunch clashes against Forest and the Scousers themselves to come. Relieved pro-establishment commentators (I think you know who this means) flocked to laud Mickey, shouting, "We told you so!" at all those who'd dared to doubt the wizard Sexton's judgement. For a month, he'd been brilliant; if only the season could have gone on past May, then perhaps his whole career could have worked out very differently. Instead, come the new term, he was back to his negligible norm, trundling through a last sorry season before Big Ron arrived, took one look at him, and promptly dumped him on Goodison.

Many years later, reflecting upon the journeyman life which took on a frantically episodic quality after he left OT, Thomas himself provided a possible explanation for both that purple patch and for his otherwise grubby form. "The pressure at United got to me; I'd go out and hit the booze until the early hours. It got to the stage where I had to get pissed before I played or I couldn't handle it. In fact, I played better with a drink inside me as I felt more relaxed." This was no hyperbole, apparently: Thomas played several games under the influence. Maybe that flashing run in spring 1980 was entirely due to him hitting upon the right combination of mixers and bottles? If so, what happened to the recipe? – for certainly by August he'd lost it again.

There's little doubt that Mickey was going to be sold by Ron a.s.a.p., in a boot sale if necessary, for packhorses who couldn't pass have never been welcomed in any Atkinson team. (Whatever Ron's failings, he could never be accused of abandoning his own footballing principles, and the teams he produced between 1981 and 1986 remain, in many Reds' eyes, as stylish as those classics of 1976 and 1994, perhaps even preferable to the side of today.) Mickey nevertheless could have tried to cling on dingleberryishly for seasons to come with his four-year deal safely tucked up in his kitbag; stupidly, he made his own noose by doing a runner as United prepared to set out on a Far East summer tour in 1981. He literally unbuckled his seatbelt and walked off the 747 to go and see the missus: not for the first or last time, the siren call of Colwyn had proved too alluring, even compared to Kuala Lumpur's. For the next decade, he'd be wandering the country in his Ford Capri Injection, listening to his Bryan Ferry tapes, transferring from one struggling club to another, interspersed with panicky flights back to North Wales. His gift for bad timing and *faux pas* would never desert him. Signing for Chelsea, he drew Ken Bates's attention to a fit young babe walking by the window and remarked that he'd like to give her one, whereupon Ken gruffly noted he was talking about his own daughter-in-law. He joined West Brom full of excitement about working under Johnny Giles only to turn up for his first training session and discover Giles had been sacked that morning. He began thriving at Chelsea and enraged us old tormentors by scoring against us at OT, only to get injured and ignominiously lose his place to Mickey Hazard. And whenever he fucked up in his private life, somehow the tabloid hounds found out every time. "May all your disgraces be private" ('Diamond' J Quimby, 1995) – how Mickey would have appreciated the sentiment behind that politician's toast.

Dribs and drabs of minor naughtiness followed Mickey throughout his career, his newsworthiness assured for evermore thanks to the adjective "ex-Red". No matter where he was hanging his boots at the time, somehow any Thomas episode reflected partially on United, as though by making him a 'star' we had to take responsibility for him for life, just as we seem to do with George Best. Finally, two 90s tabloid explosions covered Thomas with raked muck, squalid and tacky enough to make George Best look classy in comparison.

In 1992 a now balding Thomas had sloped off in his VW down a Clwyd country lane for a bit of how's-yer-father with an old childhood sweetheart, Erica Dean, who also happened to be married to his former brother-in-law. According to evidence later given in court, this had become a regular fixture in Mickey's programme but unfortunately for him, the hubbie had got hold of the fixture list. As the pair got down to some goalmouth action, Geoffrey Dean and an accomplice sprang out of the darkness, booted the window in, and proceeded to lay into the stunned Thomas. A hammer and screwdriver were produced – not, it transpired, to fix the window – and during the pulping that ensued, Thomas remembered hearing one saying, "Cut his dick off!" to which the co-defendant replied wittily, "We'll have to find it first." Rather idiotically, one of the assailants had prefaced his attack by yelling "Run, Erica, run!" thus revealing the premeditated nature of the incident and ensuring Erica got convicted too. For the tabloids, the best bit came in the detail – Thomas had been stabbed a dozen times with the screwdriver in his left arse-cheek, leading one wag to suggest Mickey had been lucky to avoid brain damage. The attackers got banged up, the only arse-bandits in nick not on Rule 43.

This had been embarrassing enough but at least Mickey had been a victim, rather than a perp: a week later, however, he would be in the dock rather than the witness box, charged with passing dud tenners. Wrexham youth players had been buying them from him for a fiver a pop and the prosecution claimed he'd passed on £840's-worth in just two months. The judge gave him 18 months, a sentence of astonishing severity, to which Thomas replied as he was taken down, "Anyone got change for a tenner for the phone?" On arrival in prison, Thomas pulled out a wad of Monopoly money to sign for warders and inmates; later, he'd make the tabloids yet again after being photographed boozing inside the nick. On one absurd occasion, he even talked warders at his open prison into taking him out for a session which ran long past lock-up time, forcing the scallies to break back into the cells before the escape alarm was raised. Clearly, ten years of duckin' 'n' divin' had toughened up the hide of a bloke who used to quake at the mere sight of Lou Macari.

I daresay Mickey would not be too pleased to be forever remembered as a counterfeit fraudster who got stabbed in the arse, run ragged by his temperamental glamour girl wife and who was seen winking shamelessly every Saturday night in front of the nation. Personally, I'll always remember him thus: however badly or boringly United are playing at any given time, all I need to do to console myself is rustle up the early teen memories of the late 70s, see the dispiriting visages of Sexton and Thomas in my mind's eye, and remind myself that nothing could be as deathly as that again. Not even Karel Poborsky.

THE
ROARING
BOYS

Alex Ferguson knew he wasn't exactly walking into a happy camp when he arrived in November 1986. Big Ron's Old Trafford empire, which only twelve months before had shimmered with golden promise as United lead the League, had been shattered into pieces and now resembled Rome after a lightning sack by the Visigoths. Indeed, much like ancient Rome, the Club had supposedly been revealed to be a decadent, orgiastic mess, all glitter and stars on the outside, but crumbling within as the corrosive effects of alcohol did their worst. The Olsen–Moses punch-up was still fresh in the tabloid memory but most observers saw that outburst, in which Remi floored Jesper with two haymakers during training, as merely a symptom of a massive underlying malaise. And the root cause, as far as the more Puritanical were concerned, was the demon drink: the Old Trafford Drinking Club had become a notorious establishment around town, a rolling roadshow featuring all United's giants such as Hughes, Robson, McGrath, Moran and Whiteside. Most of United's other alleged problems, such as failings in the scouting and youth set-ups, were fixable without undue pain – although chief scout Tony Collins would later threaten to sue Fergie over remarks the boss made in his *Six Years At United* book about the state of the Club's foundations. But tackling the cliques and cabals within the first team and the drinking culture that they shared would be far more problematic. Some, like Robson, would knuckle down and grow into an accommodation with the new Roundhead order; but McGrath and Whiteside in particular would always remain Ron's Cavaliers at heart. Ferguson would spend most of the next four years fire-fighting: struggling to keep his job but also battling to change the spirit of the Club. The tabloids, as ever, stood by ready to give succour and space to the casualties.

At least Fergie managed to get his own sordid scandal out of the way "early doors", as his predecessor would say. The *Daily Star* on the morning of 14 May 1987 decided that the imminent general election was not the national issue of the day and preferred "SOCCER BOSS FERGIE'S SECRET LOVE". Blonde 26-year-old waitress Deirdre McHardy claimed to have had an affair lasting several months with Alex behind Cathy Ferguson's back. Once gagging readers got inside, they disappointedly discovered that it had all supposedly taken place when he was at Aberdeen, though the young lady did provide a note of intrigue in the coda when she said Fergie had been back to her restaurant asking for her "only a few weeks ago". Nor, sadly, did she provide much rumpy detail beyond describing the convenient flat Fergie used two minutes away from Pittodrie. So no performance figures: compared to a classic Martin Edwards story, which never comes without black suspenders and positional descriptions, this was as frustrating as a dry hump.

Still, what must the OT mandarins have thought? United's managerships were supposed to run on a Hamlet/Joker alternation, with the former going teetotally to bed at 10 with a book, the latter metaphorically licking champagne from blondes' navels at 3 am – thus, we'd gone O'Farrell–Docherty–Sexton–Atkinson–Ferguson in strict Roundhead/Cavalier rotation. Had we all got Fergie wrong? When you read Ms. McHardy describe Fergie as "standing all suntanned and smiling on my doorstep with a bottle of vodka in hand", you had to double-check to make sure this wasn't a Big Ron story. Since that exposure, barely a word about Fergie's personal life has leaked out anywhere. Most United-based reporters would be too scared to run anything anyway. There was one ridiculous rumour about Fergie and a player's wife, said player being then accused of blackmailing the club into keeping him on instead of selling him. Complete bollocks, of course, but give journalists a few days without a good story and they start feeding off each other's crazed imaginations like you wouldn't believe.

With McGrath and Whiteside, you didn't need to use your imagination: they kept Mancunians in drinking tales for months on end. How easy it would have been for Fergie if the two had been merely decent players, instead of the legends they actually were. For make no mistake – these were two of the ten best players of the last twenty years and both were nowhere near their sell-by dates either. Nor did they suffer particularly from bad form; their only Achilles' heel was their susceptibility to injury, which the black propagandists whispered to hacks was drink-related. From the spring of 1988 until their final departures in the summer of 1989, it was rare for a month to go by without renewed transfer speculation concerning the pair. Both submitted, and then withdrew, transfer requests at various stages until Fergie finally bit the bullet and offloaded them to Villa and Everton. To a large and vocal section of the Stretford End, to whom Whiteside in particular was the cult hero of the decade, this constituted something approaching a final straw. When '89/90 began to go spectacularly pearshaped, Fergie found that by dumping the duo, he'd spent all that remained of his available credit – as far as these vocal fans were concerned.

Big Norm was a prodigiously talented player, and an equally superb drinker. Because he was never reliant on his pace, he never had to worry about the marathon sessions weighing him down – as long as the skill in his touch and the vision in his brain remained, he'd be fine. And if anything, the more his epic drinking career continued, the braver and harder a player he became. No-one who saw him take on Liverpool in April 1988 like something out of the *Dirty Dozen*, at a time when legend claimed he downed 12 pints every other night, could be in any doubt about that. Only once did any specific drinking bout hit the papers, when the *People* reported he'd been fined £3,000 for drinking champagne with the club sponsors after a match in 1988. This was a tough one for Norm, who was never well paid by United, especially as he'd only had one glass and was supposed to be in the middle of a peace plan with Fergie. (Fergie–Norm–McGrath peace plans were as bi-annual as Northern Ireland's.) He didn't actually get done for drink-driving until after he'd left United, in 1990. Four times over the limit, his undoing was his rather unfortunate method of avoiding detection – driving at 20 mph down a motorway. Safer for other road-users than bombing it at a hundred like most pissed-up footballers, but a tad easy for the police to spot as half of Cheshire queued up behind him.

Paul McGrath was slightly more accident-prone. Getting cut out of his crashed car which he'd managed to intertwine with a large oak tree when three times over the limit in November 1987 was not the sort of incident that was going to escape tabloid attention – or the court's, for that matter, who handed him a two-year ban. Then there was being seen supping other people's pintpot dregs after a riotous testimonial do – behaviour hardly likely to endear him to the Boss – though Paul later claimed it had all been a jokey misunderstanding. Or how about the time he missed the team coach to the airport on a tour of Malta because he was in the middle of a great session, thus getting stung with a hefty fine and yet another bollocking. As Paul said, it's not as if he missed the plane; but what might have passed muster under Ron worked no longer. Both he and Norm were alleged to have had two written warnings about their behaviour, innumerable face-to-face 'hairdryer' verbals and several fines for breaking pre-match 'drink curfews'. Norm would often escape attention by being slightly more subtle but Paul, typically, would get himself seen by United fans leading a conga-line with pint in hand at 2 am during an Altrincham pub lock-in. Fergie, with his spy network implanted all over the region, would always find out; in some ways, it's amazing they lasted until 1989.

The most notorious of all incidents, which almost certainly sealed their fate, occurred in the week leading up to United's Cup tie at QPR in January 1989. The Norm and Paul Roadshow had been in operation midweek; Norm was injured anyway but Paul was a possible for Saturday. Fergie and Paul dispute who told what to whom but the upshot was clear: Fergie thought Paul had drunk himself out of fitness in the 48 hours before the match, whilst Paul said he'd been told he wasn't expected to play. But what pushed a perhaps routine misunderstanding over the edge was the fact that Paul and Norm had been on Friday's *Kick Off* TV programme, appearing to be in a 'relaxed' state of mind to say the least – Fergie even phoned up Granada demanding to know whether McGrath was, in fact, pissed. Now that the matter had gone public – for most Reds watching could see something was amiss – Fergie felt he had no option but to go bollock-nuclear. The whole tale leaked out to the press. Every story's first para included "sources" claiming that Paul in particular had been told, "Stay off the booze and get fit – or quit the game." Legend has it that the argument between Fergie and McGrath an hour before the game contained more swear words than all those chanted that afternoon in the Stretford End. As McGrath's usual tactic in face-to-face confrontation was to play dumb, keep quiet and take his punishment (following the Best Method), most observers sensed that they had all crossed the Rubicon – somewhere in Old Trafford, they'd be dusting down the boys' National Insurance cards.

Bryan Robson, at least in the drink-driving stakes, managed to outdo both his companions by getting banned twice – for one year in 1982, then for three in 1988 after running out of petrol on the M62 and refusing to give any test specimens when the cops rolled up to check him out. In fact, Robson was a greater drinker than any of his contemporaries. Gordon Strachan relates a night out with Robson, when he finally realised Robbo was no mere mortal; the night ended with Strachan unconscious on his doorstep and feeling like he couldn't move for a week afterwards, only to see Robson in training next day going flat out after having drunk thrice what wee Gordon had imbibed. Another colleague once described Robbo as the "most efficient drinking machine of his generation" and no-one questioned his right to be Captain of the

Drinking Team as well as of the Football Club. You have to hope he bequeathes his body to medical science because, clearly, he should not have been able to function. He trained, Barson-style, like a demon, as if following Frank's old method to cut the calories, and played every game as though it were his last. Yet unlike Frank, he hadn't been a physical titan to start with: Robbo was terribly weedy as a young man and had to be built up by dieticians at West Brom and United. How on earth did he do it? Fergie had no idea either, shruggingly accepting that here was living proof that not all boozers ruin their football. Of course, for Fergie, Robbo was the exception that proved the rule; nevertheless, it meant he was given lee-way, as long as he didn't encourage the youngsters and didn't drink after a Wednesday if we were playing on Saturday. Robson, Big Ron's protégé and the very embodiment of United's mid-80s star-studded side, had often been seen as someone who would inevitably become a Fergie victim. But he disciplined himself sufficiently to make the transition and instead became Fergie's trusted leader in the dressing room.

Whether his gross beer intake actually lessened at all was another matter, and one his chauffeur was keen to elaborate upon in 1990. The driver who'd ferried Robbo around during his ban spilled all to the *Sunday Mirror*, who deemed it a bigger story than the London poll tax riots and thus plastered it all over the front page. And "plastered all over Cheshire" was the gist of the story, to the surprise of absolutely no Reds whatsoever. So Robbo was often so pissed "he couldn't talk, stand up or use his phone" and that sometimes, when he pulled up to his house and opened the door, "Robson would just fall out of the car": as long as he continued to perform as brilliantly as he had that season, few Reds cared. Indeed, the fact that the driver confirmed Robson's "not-after-Wednesday" golden rule and that, no matter how pissed, he always remembered to pick up the kids from school, was rather reassuring – he'd discovered how to enjoy life AND maintain his responsibilities. What fault could Fergie find with that? Even so, comically, Robson still pulled the old schoolies' trick of eating Trebor's Extra Strong Mints to hide the morning-after smell of booze from Fergie.

Admittedly, there were occasions when Robbo risked exposing more than just his fondness for the hop, such as in 1988 when, after an all-night bender in High Wycombe with Peter Shilton, he staggered into the bogs and pointed Percy only to realise that he was in the Ladies'. And, more precisely, in full sight of one dishy brunette lady called Anna Consdor. Fortunately, she took it all in good humour and later accepted a lift home from him but, given what had happened to Clayton Blackmore eight months ealier, it had been a lucky escape. With touching honesty, Robbo admitted that he'd been too utterly smashed to remember anything after last orders anyway. The *Sunday People* still thought it worth a page one banner headline "ROBBO IN FLASHING SENSATION", although surely a story claiming Robbo had been seen stone cold sober on a Saturday night would've been far more sensational. Besides, there's a long and honourable tradition of famous Reds getting their knobs out in public, as Peter Boyle will confirm...

Nowadays, Reds fans seem to have a lower tolerance threshold for the kind of high jinks that were habitual in the 80s, mainly because our standards are higher; we can afford to lambast a striker seen acting the goat in Deansgate because there's plenty of quality players who can take his place and act responsibly. Back then, our squad contained the following: Ralphie Milne, Jim Leighton, the Gibsons, Neil Webb,

Mickey Phelan, Mal Donaghy, Peter Davenport, Viv Anderson, Clayton Blackmore and Peter Barnes. A half-fit, half-cut Norman Whiteside had more to offer a match than all of those put together. Of course, we have double standards: we forgive Roy Keane for an alleged misdemeanour, but we'll slate Teddy Sheringham for something not half as bad. That's football, and that's right – players earn 'behavioural credits' on the field, which they can go and spend off it like lunatics if they so wish. In the 80s, there were no options in any event. As Paul McGrath, for example, was the only world-class defender we had, he'd have been forgiven even if he'd run down three cute kittens on the way to that tree.

The Nineties breed of Red player is generally a more strait-laced, responsible, even boring figure, but that's what makes Fergie happy. Outbreaks such as the 1991 Rotterdam coach punch-up, when Ralphie Milne (hurrah!) was struck by a flying beercan, are regrettably rare; when rumbles like the 1994 Chester "race riot" hit the front page, in which Paul Ince and Eric Cantona were at the centre of a punch-up with scally "businessmen", it tends to turn out that Reds were innocent victims rather than devilish perpetrators. Even that tabloid stand-by of the ex-Red emerging to have a pop at the Club has become a rarity. United now keep watch over their ex-players so that few make a sound. Karel Poborsky's outburst after his move to Benfica was quite shocking because we'd almost forgotten players can shout the odds in such a fashion. But in the 80s, a succession of malcontents trundled up to take on Fergie or the club: Strachan, Graeme Hogg, Billy Garton, Paul McGrath and Ralpie Milne all had their 15 minutes of dumpee-vitriol fame. Perversely, one almost misses those kinds of outbursts; these days, you only hear one side of the story, the PR-led sanitised Club view, wherein every official works their guts out, every player is a good lad, and no-one ever has a cross word or a disagreement about policy. Maybe the new order is good for the Club but who can tell? After all, if we applied the same argument to the nation's affairs as a whole, we'd be claiming that the Government should control all the media if it wants to be successful. It might be quite refreshing and illuminating to see a couple of 80s-style break-outs, to hear dumped players spilling some bile. Especially if those players were to be Teddy Sheringham and Jordi Cruyff...

THE
KNIGHT
IN SHADY
ARMOUR

Who do you think garnered the most tabloid headlines in the latter half of 1989? The Berliners bringing down their wall? Those first backbench challengers to Thatcher's premiership? The drug-crazed Madchester kids and their wacky adventures? No: I'm almost certain, judging from my bulging cuttings file, that it was Michael Knighton. And his explosion onto the front pages was even more remarkable given that no-one in the media had ever heard of him before. Such is the power of the name "Manchester United" – try and get your mitts on that and you're a national figure overnight. Poor Michael would suffer the fate of many new media-stars as they do the Dance of the Seven Veils with the tabloid caliphs, ending up skewered as the nationals' kebab. Today he runs Carlisle United, who scoot about between divisions 2 and 3, and makes the jokier sections of the tabloids with hooting UFO-related exposés and incredulous commentaries about his making himself team manager. Yet he once had the power in his hands to transform himself into British football's most important single figure, not to mention Businessman of the Decade; instead of leading his tiny club's struggle for survival in the Nationwide slums, he could be worth £200 million and spearheading United's world-wide expansion. Whatever you think of Knighton, and whatever mistakes he made during those extraordinary 1989 months, one fact remains: when the deadline came, no-one could have stopped him had he sought to enforce the deal he'd cut to buy United. No-one, that is, except Knighton himself; and he, voluntarily, against his advisors' wishes, surrendered his once-in-a-lifetime opportunity. Why? He says he did it out of honour, and those who howl in derision should consider the man's character first.

How typical of him, for example, that he has always refused to lay the blame for the humiliation United suffered at the door of the man who was really the culprit – Martin Edwards. It always puzzled me why Edwards and Knighton appeared to get on so well, for they were polar opposites in some ways, the good and bad flip sides of the 80s enterprise culture's coin. Edwards was born with a silver cleaver in his mouth, never had to struggle for anything in life and hasn't exactly acquired a reputation for Stakhanovite industriousness – he was always the kind of bourgeois overlord whose continued enrichment under Thatcherism made a mockery of that creed's claims to meritocratic legitimacy. Knighton, however, was a new kind of working-class hero; his father had been a miner, a driver and a baker, meaning Michael had to start on his own way in life with no more riches than a sound moral upbringing. Furthermore, there was no effortlessly smooth transmission to the top for Knighton – indeed, life threw a series of challenges and setbacks in his way which he overcame through daring, guts and sheer native suss.

A good player as a young man, he was forced to give up the

pro game after a serious injury. Robbed of his life ambition, he started again as a teacher after financing himself back into further education; after four years, he'd sensationally risen to be one of youngest headmasters in the country, and after seven years of scrimping sacrifice bought out the school itself. When his partially paralysed son was born, it had placed yet another challenge in his path, for a teacher's lot in the regressive 80s was not a secure one and he would need extra money for special needs – he had thus determined to become entirely financially self-sufficient and continued progressing into the property market during the 80s, selling the only family asset (the car) to raise his first deposit. Within four years, Knighton's gamble had paid off spectacularly; with little more to offer than enthusiasm, hard work and an intelligent eye for a chance, he'd become a millionaire. He'd inherited no shares, borrowed no money, relied on no old-boy networks, yet by 1989 his personal fortune stood comparison to Martin Edwards's. Moreover, he'd done it without exploiting any workers, or flogging shoddy goods like so many Ratnerised tycoons: to invert Edward Heath's famous condemnation of Lonhro, Knighton was the acceptable face of popular capitalism and enterprise.

Some of this subtext did appear to work its way into the Red public's consciousness, at least subliminally, although the immediate popular welcome for Knighton's bid was probably more rooted in him not being Martin Edwards: after all, there'd even been Reds who'd have preferred Robert Maxwell to Edwards when the fat fraudster came bouncing down Warwick Road to flirt with bidding for United in '85. Not only was Edwards loathed for a wide variety of reasons *per se*, he'd clearly signalled his intent to cash in as soon as convenient and profitable anyway – his was what the Yanks call a lame duck presidency, obviously in the last months of a final term, just seeing out the time before retiring to the farmstead. All eyes were on the succession from the mid-80s onwards, which produced a kind of strategic paralysis at Old Trafford. What did Martin Edwards achieve in the entire decade from 1980 to 1990? He launched a failed basketball club, a moribund newspaper venture and he sold Mark Hughes. Compared to United's madcap business activity in the Nineties, this looks even more pitiful in hindsight than it did then, if that's possible. Nor did there appear to be any blueprint for the future, any sign that the various expansionist ideas which surfaced from time to time were ever going to be enacted. Edwards had already told the Board he'd make his mind up about his future at the end of 1989/90. In the event, he jumped the gun by twelve months, and omitted to inform the Board that he was doing so. That fateful, and frankly stupid, decision was entirely his fault, not Knighton's, and remained the cause of much of what followed.

The day Michael Knighton emerged onto the Old Trafford pitch to score in the Stretford End goal, blow kisses to the crowd and juggle his balls might have caused cringes in the tunnel and boardroom, but is fondly remembered by those fans who were there and who can set aside 20/20 hindsight. As the team proceeded to thrash champions Arsenal 4-1 in the balmy August sunlight, we all believed we were on the cusp on a new and glorious era. Actually, we were: it just took a couple of years for the effects to work through. Long after he'd ceased to be a United director, Knighton's ideas were still paying off for the Club and fuelling Ferguson's V12 super-team.

Sadly for Michael, that interregnum claimed its human sacrifice: Knighton himself. Fans who'd polled 6-1 in his favour in August were 6-1 against by September as Maxwell set his press hounds onto him, aided by the *Manchester Evening News*. That there were major flaws in the proposed deal was obvious; Knighton himself made tactical errors and, erm, mis-statements which damaged his position and credibility. The most detailed account of these shenanigans is in Michael Crick's masterpiece *Betrayal of a Legend* where you can read about every financial blow and counter-blow. It is, however, markedly anti-Knighton in tone and analysis, so the fair-minded might prefer to wait for Knighton's autobiography due out next year in order to effect a decent compare 'n' contrast job. Although the affair left Edwards and the rest of the Board embarrassed, it would still be Knighton who got landed with most of the blame.

But the embarrassment and humiliation of which all the directors complained was largely self-inflicted. Edwards had initially met Knighton secretly without telling the other direc-tors, even though he knew that two of them would have want-ed to bid for his shares too. He then told Knighton he want-ed £20 a share for his 51 per cent stake in the club, a total of £10 million, which constituted an absolute bargain that Knighton accepted without a second's hesitation. Whilst it is true that United's share price was less than £20 at the time, there wasn't a properly free and unrestricted market in them: the share-price was not 'real' but almost nominal, and took no account of the club's obvious unrealised potential. Knighton knew, and promised, that under progressive management the Club would be worth £150 million in three to four years, a prediction at which many United cronies scoffed. But Knighton was right – indeed, he'd even underestimated the realisable growth – and there were plenty of City experts who knew he was right too. In all the furore that ensued, it's easy to forget that admiration for Knighton's savvy in the City was almost total. He'd pulled off the deal of the decade – an option to buy Britain's biggest club at a knock-down price, and he'd come from nowhere to do it. In a decade that adored tales of enterprising derring-do, this was a doozy.

Edwards's secrecy made a rod for the Board's own back. Later, director Nigel Burrows would be one of those shouting loudest about the "treachery" and clumsiness which characterised the affair, but he had wangled the truth about the bid out of Edwards very early on and for some reason agreed to maintain the secret. A couple of years later, Burrows would be disgraced and drummed out of United, having once argued in the wake of the affair that he and Amir Midani should have been allowed to buy, or at least control, the Club. If, as Michael's critics alleged, United had had a lucky escape from a Knighton regime, then I guess avoiding Burrows's clutches was even greater good fortune. Tellingly, Knighton's takeover plan envisaged the removal of Burrows from the board. Fellow directors Bobby Charlton and Mike Edelson didn't even know about the bid until ten minutes before the news was broadcast to the nation on *News At Ten*: needless to say, this exclusion did not make them happy bunnies. Edwards had managed to piss off the entire Board and, as the deal's details became public, to make himself look like a fool too – no-one could understand why he was selling so cheaply, and why he'd insisted on a secrecy that could only cost him further. For had he been open from the start, he would doubtless have kick-started an enormous auction for his stake, from which he could potentially have realised many millions more than the ten Knighton was offering.

Knighton regards Edwards as his friend and will not publicly criticise his tactics in 1989. He's suggested that Martin wanted secrecy to avoid embarrassment and a media circus over United's sale, and that he was prepared to take only £10 million because Knighton had promised to use a further available £10 million to rebuild the Stretford End. Besides, Martin had had enough: he knew the fans hated him and it was time to enjoy a quiet life, resting on the satisfying knowledge that he'd left United in good hands and with the builders in. Knighton's defence of Edwards is impressive in a game where big egos are only too eager to slag each other off and stab each other in the back. But occasionally, Michael can't help the truth slipping out. When Reds fans quizzed him on this issue recently, he wondered whether Edwards's acceptance of £10 million was a case of "not being able to see the wood for the trees". Michael could not only see the wood, but that it was prime grade mahogany too. As Knighton told us, he'd have paid £40 a share if necessary – and at £20 million for 51 per cent, he'd still have made ten times his stake within six years.

When the deal unravelled, leading to the absurd situation of Edwards having to threaten legal action against Knighton to try and lever the bleeding Board off the hook, Knighton was beseiged on all sides by accusers, hostile fans and dithering investors. Yet at that 11th hour, as his own legal advisors made clear to him, he could still have exercised his option and taken control, no matter what blustering threats were emanating from Old Trafford. Had he been more like Martin himself, or like any number of hard-faced 80s money barons, he might have dismissed his current unpopularity as a negligible hazard of the job: the world is full of companies run by monsters who are hated by both staff and customers, after all. An imminent paper profit of several millions would have been ample consolation. But Knighton has always appeared to be one of those blokes who likes to be liked; not necessarily in a smarmy, desperate fashion, but in a basic human way. It takes a special kind of breed to be able to ignore hostility and aggravation and plough on regardless – corporate Britain is full of them, and they're usually dubbed "ruthless" rather than the more accurate "bastards". Knighton decided to withdraw primarily as a personal favour to Edwards and was duly rewarded with a directorship but I also suspect he didn't have the bastard heart to take sole charge of an institution whose staff and adherents were united only by their hostility towards him. There'd be money in it, but no fun: and Knighton strikes me as a man who sees life as something to be enjoyed rather than merely enriched.

What would life have been like under Knighton instead of Edwards? Hugely bloody entertaining, naturally, but business-wise perhaps not much different given that the two were both proponents of the same blueprint. For, as some at United will occasionally grudgingly concede, Knighton left United with a set of ideas and strategies which have apparently been slavishly followed ever since. Politically, United try to play this down, giving the credit to the corporate regime instituted after flotation, but a glance through Knighton's original manifesto reveals the truth: professionalised marketing and brand exploitation; pursuit of new TV deals and revenues; an international merchandise retail network; ambitious ground redevelopment; and new leisure facilities at the ground, including a hotel. He had a fully-formed vision of what United are today and a strategic plan by which it could be achieved. That would not necessarily improve his image in some fans' eyes, who see most such developments as the work of corporate devilry, but the more sophisticated analysis is that we have not objected to these expansions being effected, merely to the manner and extent of their execution. There was an immediate and lasting impact back in 1989 too – the Knighton factor loosened Old Trafford's purse strings to a sufficient degree to enable the purchase of Pallister and Ince, crucial acquisitions in the foundation work of the success to come. Catch Knighton in the right mood and there's no mistaking the pride he feels in seeing all his hopes for United come to pass, remarkably untainted by any possible bitterness that it is Edwards and not himself who has reaped the credit and reward.

Given that MUFC plc as we know it today is at least partly of Knightonian parentage, I suppose it is conceivable that, had he closed the deal, he would have become as much of a corporate tart as the rest of the plc-wallahs. Still, I would like to think that Knighton's roots and, I think, genuine empathy for the lot of the ordinary supporter would have produced some evident results. I once asked him about his original promise in 1989 that, as chief of United, he would take no salary, merely appropriate "consultancy fees", given that his main reward would be in the increased value of his equity investment. Smartly, he immediately spotted that I was really having a dig at Edwards, tempting him to portray himself as someone who would have made a more fan-friendly chairman. He mounted a blustering defence, rising to a crescendo that Martin was "worth every penny he's ever made" in the light of what United had become. But a week later, he wrote to me and sheepishly admitted that "on reflection, whether I would have taken £30 million out [of the club] as it is alleged that Martin Edwards has done, is perhaps open to debate". I thought this was very sweet, seemingly torn between his own principles and his loyalty towards his friend, perhaps too between his roots and the circles in which he now moves. There is an awareness also of the true nature of the beast he himself had helped to unleash. Questioned by Reds about the downside of flotation and football's Brave New World – ticket prices, lack of atmosphere, players' wage inflation – he sounded unhappy and uncomfortable, offering no glib defences or easy answers. He particularly regretted the abject lack of communication between fans and administrations in general, although he was hasty to add that few fans understood the difficulties he faced, the stock chairman's answer that they're all required to parrot. That 1989 opening day farrago in front of the Stretford End may have been a smarmy, bullshitter of a stunt, and subject to immense ridicule, but underneath the crassness lay something tangible. Knighton always wanted so much to connect to "The Terrace", recognising that his Derbyshire roots and football's magic reside therein, yet he had already become part of a class within football whose continued power and status depends on the diminution and eradication of The Terrace and all it represents. You might argue that this is not much of a defence, but at least these issues appeared to matter to him. I doubt whether Martin Edwards has ever really felt anything but fear and loathing for us; the mere idea that he could even want to perform such a symbolic act as Knighton did is patently absurd. Admittedly, I doubt you'd ever see Martin captured in the press talking about close encounters of the third kind either. But then again, if aliens do exist and wanted an interesting subject to abduct, I bet they'd rather spend a space-ride in colourful Knighton's company than old Martin's...

THE
MEGA-DONS

If there's one position at Manchester United more sought after than the Captaincy, it's the unofficial title of OT Sex God – at least, ever since George Best publicised the opportunities available to a good-looking player in a red shirt. It's deeply unfashionable and un-PC to say so in this post-Hornby era but Manchester has always been full of sad slappers who dream of shagging as many footballers as possible. Whether they're in it for the cash, the kudos, or just the chance to get a ride on a proper athlete instead of some Salford scrote, any half-decent looking player is never going to go short of horizontal training. And if you happen to belong to 'glamorous' United, and are a bit of all right in the hunk stakes, you barely need to bother looking for it. It comes to you gift-wrapped, at any hour of the day or night you fancy. Just look out for those hidden tape-recorders, lads.

From the mid-80s until the rise to superstardom of Ryan Giggs, there were two Reds topping the Carnal Countdown: Clayton Blackmore and Lee Sharpe. Sad seedy figures they may be today, of course: Clayton, for example, shocked many of us when he re-emerged with Boro because he is clearly going bald. When it rains, in fact, he looks like a degenerate monk. We were horrified, because bald spots afflict fat Stretford Enders, not immortal sex gods. Could this really be the same hunk who once wowed a thousand disco-dollies? Where's the famous suntan gone, too? Surely Boro are paying him enough to maintain his solarium rental? Sharpe, who's admittedly rarely seen outside a treatment room, is still only 26 but the elfin figure and vulpine visage of the Madchester era are long gone. Bad enough that he plays for the Leeds sheepshaggers, as unsexy an outfit as you can imagine, but where's all that heavy-limbed sloth come from? How did he let his succession of drop-dead cool haircuts collapse into an upsetting disaster zone? He may, theoretically, be worth £5 million but to your average 16-year-old Manc nymph, he's long past his sell-by date. Gone are the days, so fondly remembered, when you could enter a Lee Sharpe Fan Club do at the Royale and be overwhelmed by the stench of raging teenage hormones and juices. Here was a boy who once faced the possibility of a virgin shag on the hour every hour for the rest of his life. Oh, how the mighty are fallen. And they were never really replaced; Giggs and Beckham are, appallingly, settling down when they should be entering a golden era of oats-sowing whilst the other fledglings are too boring or ugly to trouble the scorers.

As for Clayton, the only boring thing about him was his playing style; he was never going to win any Supporters Player of the Year Awards. Flitting in and out of the side between 1984 and 1994, he only amassed about 200 appearances, though he does have the distinction of having played in every shirt number from 2 to 11. Yes, there were plenty who said

Clayton was a man of many positions, fnar fnar. And it was his personal habits, rather than his mediocre blunderings around the field, that attracted most attention. Within months of arrival at OT from some bestial part of Wales, he'd had a complete makeover. Gone was the horrific wispy moustache and fright-wig bubble-perm that had made him look far too Scouse for comfort. In their place came a classic matinee-idol side-parting, from which not a hair ever seemed to be dislodged, prompting suggestions of substance-abuse i.e. hairspray. Not a trace of stubble would ever be seen again on his chiselled jawline nor, so it sometimes appeared, on his legs. Those thighs, impressively sculptured though they were, did seem suspiciously smooth. Perhaps it was the effect of the tan, a bronzing of all-year-round depth that became his most famous feature. So blatantly not a consequence of Mancunian climes, his subsequent nickname stuck forever: "Sunbed". Never would you see Clayton in a fanzine cartoon without dark shading and wrap-around Raybans – he was the epitome of Eighties naff-cool, someone you'd expect to say "baby" every other sentence and perhaps do extra-work in Wham! videos on his days off. He was, as they say, "mega": more on that adjective's amusing subtext later.

Meanwhile, an urban legend was born. Clayton-on-the-pull stories were legion, as he was sighted at every shlocky Manchester niterie, firing off that famous dazzling smile in an ambience of cocktails, Duran Duran singles and white stilet-toes. And why not? He was single, well off and in the peak of condition. If shag-marathons were indeed the order of the day for Clayton, it was certainly doing his football some good, for he developed thigh power of such frightening intensity that few goalkeepers dared touch his free kicks. When Clayton's blaster virtually won us the Cup Winners Cup by getting us through a tricky quarter, we should have said a silent thank you to all those anonymous babes for their services to the club. Then, as crushing as Valentino's death to some, the unthinkable happened. As 1987/88 kicked off, Clayton got married. The Smiths had split the month before. It's hard to say which shocked the city more.

Naturally, Clayton had chosen a beautician, Jackie. Just because he was hitched, he obviously wasn't going to let himself go; what better than an in-house assistant for that overall tan control, hair removal, general buffing up and other essential upkeep? Clayton would continue to present himself as immaculately as ever to the OT crowd, and the Legend of the Sun King lived on.

In December '87, however, it looked for a while as though the only pump-action Clayton would be getting in the future would be with him on the receiving end. Incredulous Mancunians opened their morning papers to read that the Sunbed had been arrested and was being held overnight in a Bermudan jail as United's mini-tour went off the rails. There were plenty of Reds out there, including a *Red Issue* editor, taking advantage of the tour to escape their families for a while, who phoned back some extraordinary tales gleaned from close-quarter encounters with the players. The only one we can print, however, is as it appeared in every tabloid: Clayton had been accused of rape. The alleged victim was, inevitably, another beautician; it seems nothing beats that white-coated tweezer action once you've had a taste. 21-year-old Patricia Savoy, an American, had been at the Oasis nightclub where several United players were drinking. A five-foot, seven-stone brunette, she claimed Clayton had followed her into the ladies' at 3 am and given her one without her consent. Clayton would be spending thirty-seven hours in the slammer, with the ultimate fear of seven years to follow. We knew it was serious because Club brief 'Mo Mo' Watkins was on his way to Bermuda. We're used to seeing him on TV these days as a general plc mouthpiece but pre-flotation, any sight of Watkins out of his coffin was rare, and inevitably meant trouble. Any journalist seeing him about would know immediately to start phoning around hospitals, checking to see if any drunken international footballers had fallen through their doors.

Savoy made it sound deadly when she spoke to the press: "My life has been shattered. I am living a nightmare. No-one will ever know what I have suffered, and am still suffering." Back home, hacks swarmed around wife Jackie in her Swinton home, as she put on a brave face and declared her support for new hubby Clayton. Dad Colin made what later looked to be an insightful observation: "Footballers are sadly vulnerable to claims concocted by people who want to create scandals." But for a day, a tornado of a scandal circled barely moments from United and Blackmore: no-one could recall a major footballer being charged with rape whilst still playing, and the story looked set to dominate for weeks.

Suddenly, the charge disappeared. Clayton staggered out of his cell into the Bermudan sunlight after being told he was free to go. A statement issued by the police said: "Our inquiries are now complete and, on the advice of the Attorney-General, no person will be charged." The prospect of Clayton's entire sexual history being examined in a trial had vanished, much to the disappointment of the more blood-thirsty amongst Reds and press. A relieved wife back home whooped: "I'm so happy – I never had any suspicions." And the Manchester solarium industry held celebratory parties.

Mystery surrounded the circumstances of the decision to

release Clayton, however, which rather unfairly left a stain on his reputation. The police refused to confirm that Ms. Savoy had actually withdrawn the complaint. But Savoy herself said she had indeed done so and, remarkably, cited Jackie Blackmore as the reason for her volte-face. Said Savoy: "I felt sorry for her...I put myself in her position," a rather unfortunate phrase when you think about it. Moreover, she added, "I didn't feel I could cope emotionally with the enquiries" but still that "by asking the police to withdraw, that doesn't mean I withdraw the statement I made." And in that messy, unsatisfactory position – a kind of prosecutorial *nolo contendere* – poor Clayton was left looking like Bill Clinton (whom he kind of resembles anyway, don't you think?). He was in a limbo created by accusers who were willing to wound but not kill. Local bigwigs growled, suspecting cover-up: "There's unrest about the affair. The feeling is that because he was a famous footballer and a case would bring embarrassment to his club, proceedings were dropped," grouched Liberal MP Austin Thomas.

A bemused Clayton scampered home, with his tail or some other organ between his legs. Whilst protesting his innocence, he did confess that "I have learned again that things can get distorted. It has been a lesson to me...I will be very careful how I socialise in future. United can do without this sort of publicity." Interesting use of the verb "socialise", some wags contended: "Do you fancy coming back to my place for a bit of socialising upstairs" might have threatened to replace the old coffee ploy. In fact, few were prepared to believe that Clayton could have been in any way the kind of guy to rape someone.

Whatever lessons Clayton learned appeared to be rather quickly forgotten. At the climax of his greatest season in Red,

1990/91, it seems Blackmore let the adulation go to his head, or at least to some appropriate body-part. In the run-up to our European Final – the tabloids displaying their usual impeccable sense of timing – the *News of the Screws* plastered Clayton all over page three, a location with all the right Sunbed connotations in itself. "SOCCER STAR PLAYS AWAY WITH BLONDE", screamed the sub-ed with an utter lack of originality (and "star" was putting it a bit strong, too.) "Busty blonde barmaid" Kay Richardson had spilled all in time-honoured, hell-hath-no-fury-like-a-scorned-mistress fashion. For the paper alleged that not only had Clayton, a married man who'd "learned his lesson", shagged the night away with Kay in Portland Hotel Room 130, he'd previously told the foam-puller that he'd split from his wife. "It had been the most wonderful three hours of my life," beamed Kay; but she was to be less happy when she next caught sight of Clayton down the disco, with his wife in tow. Before she had a chance to speak/scream/slap, Clayton had whipped his arm around her and whispered, "We'll have to get together again." The outraged barmaid declared to the *Screws* that she was revealing all in the public interest – "I want to warn other girls what a rat he really is" – which was very civic-spirited of her.

So far, so amusing. But the best bits lay in the detail. Clayton's supposed plea to Kay when she told him she was going to blab was, "It's not just me you'd be hurting. It's the Club and every footballer." Brilliant! Selfless professional solidarity to the end. Far more embarrassing, however, was Kay's report of Clayton's shag-frenzy catch-phrase. For she alleged that throughout their encounter, which followed an initial pull at – of course – the Disco Royale, Clayton kept repeating, "This is mega, this is mega." Wonderful: he may well have been "gentle, with a cheeky twinkle in his eye", but from now on, Clayton would be immortalised amongst supporters as "Mr Mega". Every cartoon, every reference, evey picture that would henceforth appear in a fanzine had to have the word "Mega" in there somewhere. It was terrace law. Wherever he surfaced in public, you could hear Reds sniggering behind their hands, muttering, "Mega, mega" as he blushingly walked by. How he must have yearned for the old days, to be associated with nothing more embarrassing than daily usage of sunbeds.

Sadly, Clayton faded away after this latest incident. His last season as a regular ended in the catastrophe of United getting caught by Leeds, and he was a rare sight on the pitch after that, being finally replaced by top-notch players. But he was missed off the pitch too: Clayton wasn't the lad about town anymore, having been definitively replaced as fanny-magnet by both Sharpe and Giggs. Presumably, his wife was now keeping him on a much tighter leash – not that he'd have wanted to stray anyway, we hasten to add. The Nineties wasn't really his style of decade and besides, he was clocking on a bit now. No, Madchester and the new era demanded a very different kind of cheesecake. And Lee Sharpe was just the boy to provide it.

*   *   *

There was a time, around the middle of the 1990/91 season, when you could believe that Lee Sharpe walked on water. Now, of course, he'd have trouble floating in the Dead Sea. But as United headed for two Cup finals that year, evidently on the cusp of greatness, no-one represented this burgeoning, thrilling renaissance more than the scrawny 19-year-old winger. Suddenly, United were glam again, sharp in more than mere logo, too sexy for their shirts: we were in tune with our city, at last. For Lee Sharpe was Madchester's Red. Images of the era? The lights at the Hacienda, baggy T-shirts and fringes, and Lee Sharpe in our psychedelic blue away kit scoring a glorious hat-trick at Highbury. Eventually Madchester turned sour, and Sharpe went to pot; cultural synchronicity to the end. But if you were at Arsenal to witness that epic 6-2 demolition, or at OT to see Lee destroy Sunderland singlehandedly in February, you'd have had no doubts – Sharpe was set to become a United legend. Ryan Giggs was still just a twinkle in a reserve team coach's eye. Yet by 1994, Giggs had taken everything that once was Sharpey's; his pace, his place, his seemingly assured legendary legacy. And when the idiots at Leeds dropped £5 million into a stunned Fergie's lap for him in '96, few mourned his departure. The lads' favourite of '91 had become that most despised of creatures by then – the girlie's choice, more famous for his looks and dances than his effort or goals. And even then, he was running a poor fourth to Ryan, Becks and Eric in the stud stakes. In some ways, it's an even sadder demise than another mid-20s premature ejaculation, George Best's, for at least Best won medals and forged an eternal collective memory. Because Lee missed so many key moments through injury, then spoiled what came after with bad form and attitude, he'll never be associated with the '90s triumphs in the way that Eric, Hughes or Schmeichel are.

Fittingly, it was Best himself who stepped into the tabloids to warn Lee of the temptations ahead in 1991. Sharpe had been the sensation of the season and won the PFA Young Player Award but stories were already beginning to circulate. These were the same stories that endeared him to the Stretford End to begin with; that Lee was possibly too much of a Madchester boy for his own good. The *Daily Mirror* subhead over Best's admonitory story put it thus: "Don't Blow It Like I Did, Lee – No Birds, No Booze, No Drugs." Jeez, one might just as well have added "No Life".

After the 80s decade of naff, wherein footballers' misbehaviour generally involved very tacky 'discotheques', drunkenly driven 'executive motors' and seedy extra-marital affairs, Lee exemplified the new trendiness. You wouldn't catch him shagging barmaids, crashing Mercs and swanning about in sports casuals with Clayton. He wore what we wore, inhabited the same Madchester clubs and dated the rather classy models we'd all rather have than some slapper from Droylsden. Nor, unusually, did you ever see him smashed out of his head. Well, not on booze anyway. He was a typical young Lad, getting the best out of a city at its most vibrant, and as long as the football remained stellar, we doffed our (Henri Lloyd) hats to him. Naturally, it would be a rather different reaction when the crosses and goals dried up...

Babes all over town were willing to drop their knickers for him at the first sight of that trademark pearly-white grin. No doubt, he was the most cheekily handsome player United had had in a decade, always topped by the latest cutting-edge hairdo. Smart business advisers opened the Lee Sharpe Fan Club, the most successful of its kind in British football since Bestie's day, allowing thousands of pubescent girlies to exchange pornographic fantasies about the boy and scream each other deaf at LSFC social functions. United's merchandising department, which had just come under the wing of the self-proclaimed "genius" Eddie Freedman, thanked God for the opportunity and turned out duvet-covers by the thousand. If only they could have marketed a Lee Sharpe dildo, they'd have made enough to rebuild the Main Stand.

But it was the "no drugs" part of Best's entreaty that drew

the most attention. Madchester was fuelled by cannabis first, then E, before Gunchester's coke took over. To be under 21 and drug-free in 1990 Manchester was unusual. In a neat reversal of 60s stereotypes, it was the clean-living kids we called freaks and weirdoes; in some clubs, if you weren't rolling, sniffing or smoking something, you stood a good chance of being fingered as a nark. (Alright, I'm exaggerating, but not by much. How else to explain the early success of Northside, if not to excuse us by saying we were all too off our faces to know any better?) So when Lee started suffering injury problems, most infamously the mysterious "viral infection" that actually turned out to be meningitis, it wasn't too surprising that the terrace gossip began to solidify almost to the stage where newspapers dared suggest Lee enjoyed more than the odd pint, bird and boogie. They never quite did so, and it would be Lee himself who finally put such suspicions into print with his own secretly recorded mouth, but everyone understood the K-Stand wags who smirkingly reminded us that you spell "Sharpe" with an "E".

One fact was beyond dispute, however – that Lee was a party animal *nonpareil*. Fate chose a bad moment to reveal this to the tabloid-reading wider public: the dreadful Spring of Discontent in April 1992. United were in the midst of throwing away a title we'd been waiting a quarter of a century for and we'd hit a new low on Easter Monday, beaten 2-1 at home by Forest. Neil Webb had already disgraced himself during the 90 minutes and within 90 hours, Sharpe and Giggs would join Fatboy in the doghouse. Ferguson, quite rightly, had imposed a draconian curfew on the players that night, telling them not to leave their homes as the team had to play at Upton Park on the Wednesday night in a make-or-break crunch match. But Sharpe and Giggs bombed off to

Blackpool for a wild night of partying, cretinously believing Fergie wouldn't find out. As many players before and since have discovered to their cost, Alex Ferguson has a spy network that is the envy of MI5. The day after the catastrophic defeat at West Ham, in which both Sharpe and Giggs played mediocre parts, one of the manager's secret agents reported the Blackpool sightings to the boss, whose nose promptly went nuclear-red. He hared round to Sharpe's house for a confrontation and, jaw-droppingly, discovered another minor shindig in progress, starring Sharpe, Giggs and some youth team lads. One confessed that they were "on their way out" again, which wasn't a judicious phrase to put into Fergie's mind at such a moment, especially as Liverpool away was coming up. Had the incident occurred five years earlier, the lads involved may well have found themselves "on the way out" for good. Instead, Fergie dropped Sharpe immediately, judging him to be the Pied Piper of town-painting, and fined the two first-teamers a total of twenty grand. It was lucky for Sharpe that the full story didn't leak out until mid-May because, on the evening of 26 April after losing 2-0 at Anfield and the title, there'd have been many a Red prepared to lynch him for dereliction of duty.

Ryan Giggs seemed to learn something from the episode. Although he's racked up far more tabloid coverage than Sharpe this decade, it has rarely been of any substance. It seems every babe he's ever pulled has shagged 'n' told to the red-tops, and every time a distant relative misbehaves it makes page one. Only the 1997 Davinia Murphy story carried any real danger or proper public interest. Lee's actually had it easier; any Red-about-town can tell you eyebrow-raising stories about him that never got near the press. In some ways, he was fortunate – his laddish peak was before the papers started to overdose on football, when a story had to have real balls to make the presses. Nowadays, football is the new rock 'n' roll, and the tabs want Paul Gascoigne on the cover instead of Keith Richards or John Lydon. In 1998, three Liverpool players refusing to give a waiter a tip is deemed of sufficient newsworthiness to make a national tabloid, an absurd state of affairs. Sharpey can, perhaps, still be grateful for some consolations of early decline.

Mind you, the *Daily Star* was always embarrassingly desperate, hence their decision to stick poor Lee on the front of their rag a year later under the heading "What A Lovely Pair Of Shiners", perhaps the most wit-free and boring tabloid shoutline of the year. Lee had appeared at a charity function with Take That (a perfect association, of course) sporting two humungous black eyes which he claimed were the result of a golfing accident. (Yes, how often you see the likes of Tiger Woods and Greg Norman on TV sporting facial injuries: a completely convincing cover story...) As the *Star* suggested, far more likely that he had indeed been in a fight outside Coco Savanna's nightclub in Stockport. A staff member was quoted thus: "Lee was confronted by several young men as he left. Fists were flying...Sharpe was on the deck with blood on his face. But the police arrived in minutes." Oh dear, oh dear. Golden rule for pros out and about – never let the police get involved. Getting set upon in Manchester niteries is a hazard that goes with the job – even civilians are lucky to go a month without a good street punch-up – but once Plod arrives, it's on the record and carries incalculable potential dangers in terms of charges and court proceedings. Fergie was reported by the *Star* to be "fuming", presumably not for the act itself (United players get into rumbles all the time) but for the possible public consequences. As it happened, Sharpe escaped any ramifications, but it was still one more tabloid headline, perhaps another nail in the coffin as far as the Boss was concerned. He likes his young men married, sober and in bed by 10 pm rather than randy, up-for-it and on the streets at 3 am.

Between 1994 and 1996, Lee slipped steadily out of the Old Trafford picture. Indeed, by 1996 Lee's image was beginning to resemble a footballing Dorian Gray. Off the field, with his modelling, clothing contracts and clubbing, he was still fresh-faced young Lee with his dazzling smile, easy charm and limber gait. But on those increasingly rare occasions when his portrait came out of the attic and onto the pitch, he was a very different sight: sluggish, no longer able to trick his way past full-backs, his mind a second behind everyone else's, his passes wayward. He looked haggard, old, unhappy: the terrace cracks about his nocturnal activities were no longer good-spirited but increasingly malicious. There was a bloke in West Upper who simply used to shout, "Druggie! Druggie!" at him when he messed up; a foul calumny, doubtless, but an indication of where sentiment was heading. There was no wit or banter in the crowd's relationship with him anymore, just brooding resentment. And the new stories in the press about his exploits, which were small beer anyway, no longer concerned us as much as his ill-judged forays into 'proper' football interviews, wherein he would harp on about not being able to play the position he wanted, and how this was preventing his re-emergence into the England team. Reds growled at such insolence: to many, he was lucky to be getting into the United team in any position at all, let alone be playing left-wing for England. At a club very sensitive to the Club versus Country issue (which is to say, put United first or you're a traitor), such media meanderings were doing him little good in the fans' eyes. His unsmiling grumpiness on the bench at

Middlesbrough when we clinched the '96 title was widely deemed to be petulant and self-absorbed and drove several more nails into a coffin now nearly ready for cremation.

As far as Fergie was concerned, that cremation date must have been brought forward several months by the story that appeared in the *News of the Screws* in Ferbruary 1996. At last, all those rumours about Sharpe's supposed recklessness with babes and blow came to one concentrated head. Lindsay Pender, an 18-year-old blonde who was supposedly working on a Manchester drugs story with a *Screws* hack, was an ex of Sharpe's "from years ago" (which, if you think arithmetically, suggests one or two rather lurid headlines in itself). Lindsay and the hackette were hanging about in a notorious Manchester watering hole when Sharpe came in on the pull with Mike Summerbee's son Nicky. (Nicky at the time was struggling at Manchester City but had already acquired a reputation for, um, 'good living' of which his 60s socialite father would've been proud.) The quartet retired to Lindsay's hotel room whereupon the lads cracked open the bubbly and delightedly fell upon the TV's porn channel – allegedly, an invitation from Sharpe to progress to a life-imitating-art foursome then followed, which the ladies declined. Fatefully, the conversation turned to the enjoyment of life (getting-off-your-face sub-section), during which Lee displayed an impressive awareness of drug terminology and know-how. So far, so deniable, but declaring that his post-career aim was "to buy a yacht and sail around the Caribbean smoking a foot-long joint" was not exactly the sort of thing you'd see in a United programme pen-picture. Lee's response when the *Screws* phoned to tell him publication was imminent almost made you feel sorry for him: "You've got me by the bollocks. I need to speak to the Gaffer and my parents. My mum will have a fit." How sweet to be worried about a spanking from his mother! And if he thought his mum would have a fit, how on earth did he think Fergie would react? Now there's a meeting of which many would have liked a wall-fly view.

Now Lee's at Leeds, where bitter is king and where grass isn't what you smoke but what your lover eats. You still hear the odd Sharpe story but when he lost the Red shirt, he lost much of his news value and glamour. Those stories that have made the prints have been rather tedious girlfriend news mixed in with the occasional alleged banning from some nightclub or other. The Lee Sharpe Fan Club was wound down with almost indecent haste when it became clear he was departing Old Trafford and he's no longer quite the hot commercial sponsorship item he once was. One would hope that the cannabis revelations haven't hurt his marketability too much because, of all the alleged misbehaviour associated with Sharpey, smoking the odd joint would have been the least worrying of all sins. What really annoys fans is players staying out until all hours on the eve of a match, or always being pissed to the detriment of their fitness, or doing something politically and ethically unacceptable like publicly supporting the Tories or beating up women. Plenty don't approve of players snorting coke either, which is seen as flashily elitist and unacceptably performance-enhancing – not to mention the fact that any footballer on coke (a breed easy to find in city centres) behaves like an insufferably arrogant bullshitting tosser. Perhaps that's why so many players get into rucks with the 'civvies' – they behave like such utter Gallagheresque arseholes that a smack in the mush is the only appropriate response. But sitting on a boat in the Med, weeding away the summer, is a lovely image and entirely 'safe'; better that than drunken brawling in Dublin bars on pre-season tours.

But football has demonised cannabis and hung lads out to dry for indulging, exploiting the unfortunate property of the drug remaining detectable for weeks. Meanwhile, leading wankers at almost every Premiership club spend their early midweek nights snorting Charlie, acting like twats and evading FA detection because the drug traces disappear so easily. Lee wasn't always too clever; he let dangerous things slip into and out of his mouth; he let his game stagnate; his goal celebrations were incredibly gauche; but he was essentially a nice, good lad who loved life and treated the supporters he met out and about as equals, not supplicants. And for a year or so in our younger lives, he was the next Prince of Old Trafford. Those who were there and remember those days will never think too harshly of this Red Devil. But don't be coming back now, Lee...

THE
DIEU
AS
DIABLE

Is Eric Cantona the greatest Red Devil of them all? Probably. I'm 30, so I never saw George Best play in anger. But Eric was far and away the most brilliant, exciting and important player I've ever seen in a Red shirt. He's included in this book for fairly obvious reasons, the infamous kung-fu kick being merely the most notorious. This isn't the place to recall the galaxy of stellar moments he provided on the pitch – by definition, we're here to talk about the so-called dark side. For the full picture, you might care to look at my biography of Eric, of which what follows is a taste. And even this is not bitter, but bitter-sweet; for even when he was being a bad lad, he somehow emerged with his immortality enhanced. Some trick: some Red Devil.

In the matter of Eric Cantona's record of violence, the brutal fact is that a large proportion of his following admired and approved of his 'hardness' and his ultimate willingness to express his anger physically. Not that Eric is essentially a violent man; not for him the routine Saturday night thuggery exhibited by some of his contemporaries, nor does his speech contain the tiresome threatening macho swagger of so many 90s Lads. Indeed, the hoariest old Eric quote is the one about passion and fire harming him and others; he is no apologist for brutality.

Nonetheless, he has a track record of bundles which are detailed below. The classic intellecto-pacifist argument would be that if Eric is supposed to be so sensitive, intelligent and self-possessed, resorting to violence is in fact an admission of inadequacy. That perhaps ignores the centrality of the instinctive spontaneity in Eric's character which can seize the initiative before the brain can engage. But on a more basic level, those on the receiving end have often asked for it and been given a taste of the only language they understand. Sorry to sound like a taxi-driver there but rational intellectual responses can be pointless when dealing with pond-life (cf. Selhurst Park, Pasadena Rose Bowl). So here are Eric's greatest hits, complete with advocate's defence.

1978: During an under-13s match at Auxerre, young Eric has a running battle with a particularly Vinnyish defender; after a gruesome hack from behind, Eric explodes and an apparently vicious fist-fight ensues which has the staff worried about his temperament for weeks afterwards. Eight years later, the protagonists meet again in a first-team Auxerre-Nantes match: both are in the bath well before time.

Defence: too young to be held criminally responsible anyway. Provocation. And you always get let off for a first-time offence, right?

1983: The infamous Magnificent Seven Massacre. It

appears players are just as susceptible as fans to seeing a car park as a fight-ring *manqué*. After an Auxerre reserve match, seven opponents wait for the home team's star at the car park entrance. Despite being warned of Eric's shoot-out prowess by Sheriff Guy Roux, the seven stand their ground, doubtless expecting the coward's odds to favour them with victory. Instead, Eric emerges in a whirlwind of kung-fu kicks and karate chops, flooring four of them within five seconds and putting the others to flight. A groundsman observer is said to have remarked with bewildered approval as the injured four sloped off to the club infirmary: "If I'd seen that in the cinema, I wouldn't have believed it."

Defence: Doesn't even warrant a reference to the CPS. Self-defence and the use of minimum necessary force in doing so; had he been in uniform, would have merited some sort of medal.

1987: Eric shows his generally overlooked humility by mucking in with the young lads and apprentices to clear the snow from Auxerre's pitch. Bruno Martini, the goalkeeper and French international club star, is standing around doing little, a fact upon which Eric remarks. Martini drops a spleen-load of abuse on Eric's head, to which Eric replies with a swift right-hander to the eye socket.

Defence: a routine event at any English club. Provocation if Madame Cantona was mentioned. Worth no more than a fine, m'lud, which is exactly what he got: Guy Roux would make a better magistrate than Mrs. Pearch, perhaps.

1989: The oft-repeated rumour is that Eric once punched Marseilles president Bernard Tapie at the climax of a heated, personal argument involving much mutual insult. Eric was on his way within days, adding to the circumstancial evidence, and their loathing of each other is well-documented. Tapie is notorious for his gigantic mouth which has got himself into plenty of trouble so you can hazard a guess that whatever he said to Eric was at a Simmonds-level.

Defence: No proof anything happened. Almost certain provocation and possibly a pre-emptive strike. And given the state of the relationship between Tapie and the French judiciary, no *juge d'instruction* would ever let a Tapie complaint proceed anyhow. Not that he could afford to press the case anymore either, tee-hee.

1990: Tough September days at Montpellier as Nicollin's dream team fails to click. In the dressing room, Jean Claude Lemoult remarks to a team-mate behind Eric's back that it's all the striker's fault. Eric swirls round and clumps his boots into Lemoult's face, sparking an all-in brawl. His Stade de Mosson days seem numbered as half-a-dozen players sign an anti-Eric round robin but all is resolved with a smacked bottom and fine.

Defence: Lemoult was possibly asking for it by questionning a proud professional's application behind his back but the use of boots as a weapon is hard to wriggle out of; blame heat-of-moment instinct and throw oneself at judge's mercy. Fortunately, French cases take aeons to come to judgment; in the meantime, Lemoult and Eric became pals so any proceedings would have been terminated by a cooked-up joint plea of "we were just horsing about / he accidentally headbutted my Reeboks" etc.

1991: Threw ball at referee's legs whilst playing for Nîmes: scarcely violent and something even saintly Ray Wilkins

enjoys doing. Should be "Case dismissed". But, just as he discovered in 1988 when calling French boss Hidalgo a "shitbag"
(and thus receiving a one-year international ban), the French
footie establishment hates its rebels even more than Lancaster
Gate does. Jacques Riolaci tells Eric he's getting singled out
for exemplary punishment; Eric responds by walking up to
each committee member and hissing, "Idiot!" in their faces.
Verbal, rather than physical, violence, but no less enjoyable.

1994: Immovable – and intensely annoying – object meets
irresistible force at the Pasadena Rose Bowl. Completely over-
the-top jobsworth security at the World Cup so enrages the
entire media that most are only too pleased when Eric gives
one a slap for refusing to let him get on with his commentary
job.
    Defence: A clear case of the only language officious pedants
understand. In any case, L.A. is the last place a jury is going
to take the word of their notorious law-enforcers over that of
a celebrity football player, right, OJ?

So when Eric arrived at United, leaving a sulphurous trail
behind him, it seemed to many that it would only be a matter of time before his nature caught up with him. The spring
of 1994 felt grim enough at the time: little did we realise that
it was only a staging post *en route* to unimaginable infamy...
    Our Caesar Cantona's Ides Of March had been pressaged at
Norwich: a bit of studs-up malarkey brought forth venom
from Jimmy Hill, who took a verbal slapping from Fergie in
reply. It wasn't to be a one-off.
    Swindon '94 was a weird day out. A tin-pot club who'd
dreamed all season about this match decided to stage it as a
Leeds '71 revival. Swindon's players combined some fairly

intelligent play with an array of shirt-pulls, tugs and sly knocks in best old-Tyke style. When Eric snapped mid-way throught the second-half, it was the classic existentialist response to the absurd world of injustice.

It wasn't actually that bad a stamping, more of a theatrical tread; looking at Eric's leg musculature, one can imagine his full force bringing forth geysers of guts and intestine. Maybe it was the complete transparency and honesty of it that shocked. There was no attempt at disguise or justification, no sneaky wait for a referee's averted gaze, just the instinctive rage of an artist rejecting society's codes of normality. Perhaps Van Gogh was in a similar kind of bate when he cut his own ear off? "Typical Dutchman," Lawrie Sanchez would no doubt have sneered.

With tabloid newsprint supplies not yet exhausted, there was room left for yet more triple-page spreads four days later after Eric stalked off at Highbury. The fact that the second yellow card for innocently colliding with Winterburn was patently unjustified scarcely mattered. Even Arsenal players coming to Eric's defence was deemed suitable only for tenth paragraph asides. A Royal Pardon would not have been enough to deflect the tabloid mission to plunge the dagger into Caesar's back. After all, they had waited many months for this chance to demonstrate that the self-appointed experts had been right from the off – this "Gallic" was trouble, too arrogant and too individualist. A five-match ban, dubbed "lenient" by the rope-twirling lynch-mob, might as well have been seven, for a wounded Eric was not all there at Wembley and against Liverpool. He would later return in a Julian triumph, the jackanapes bound in chains behind him; but we had all witnessed a chilling exhibition of what lay in wait for Eric next time he transgressed the codes of conformity.

On the night of 26 January 1995, the exhibition opened for business. (Apologies for any sense of deja vu).

And so to the moment of madness, the resurrection of Bruce Lee, the defining image of the season or whatever other label you like. Reds at Selhurst Park were still taking their post-lavatorial seats when a ball from our left looped limply over the heads of Eric and his marker/assassin Richard Shaw. Seconds earlier, Shaw had fouled Eric for the third time and gone unpunished once more. As the ball passed by, Eric extended a mildly petulant leg which, if it actually caught Shaw, could have done no more harm than a breath of summer breeze. Shaw appeared to hesitate, mid-air, for several seconds before apparently realising that the Oscar season was upon us.

Our stand was imbued with resignation rather than shock. After all, it had been six months since Eric's last dismissal and our knowledge of English refs is such that we knew a red card was well overdue. We watched from a position directly opposite as Eric traipsed down the touchline with Norm 'Munster' Davies in half-hearted pursuit. If only he'd set off alongside him…

Everyone I've spoken to since all had their eyes fixed on Eric. We saw what the TV cameras missed and what few cameras captured. Some lone lout, hardly the type that's supposed to be in a family stand, hurtles several rows down to the front. His nastily naff leather-jacket is unmistakable from even 70 yards – we are watching a creature from low down the food chain. He crosses 'the line' – not necessarily a physical mark on the ground but that boundary which we all recognise, the one that separates the players' universe from ours. He's in the 'no-man's-land' behind the hoardings, as close to the pitch as is possible without actually invading it, yet still a location in which a fan's presence would guarantee official intervention at any other ground. From our vantage point, he appears to be leaning over, inches from Cantona's face – he could be carrying a knife or bottle but a steward feet away does nothing. Someone shouts near me, "What's he throwing?" To us, it looks as though some sort of attempted assault is in preparation – but by the lout, not Eric. Norm chugs up at last, pulling Eric away and we think: "It's all over"...then something snaps within the mind of the genius and a hundred front pages are born. You've seen the rest.

*   *   *

Defiant was Eric himself: that there was no public apology following Selhurst Park and no *mea culpa* PR spread in the tabloids was typical Cantona. As with past incidents, an act that was seen objectively by outsiders as a mistake drew no regretful explanations from Eric. Many French observers have noted, often with approval, that he is simply too proud to do so – instead he assumes responsibility for his actions and takes whatever comes silently like an existential hero. Did Cantona's demeanour during '95 not recall that of Mersault in *The Outsider*? Many assume that Eric's pride still conceals a fundamental regret. But is that regret – he was reported by Fergie to be "devastated" the next day – more for the consequences and the harm done to friends than for the act itself? Many who spoke to Eric in the aftermath said he felt that he had done nothing morally wrong; the damage had been to his image, not his soul.

Two Cantona quotes help lead us towards an explanation:

"He who has regrets grimaces in the mirror when he wakes. He is a traitor to others – and above all he is betraying himself."

"Whatever people say, no-one will make me change; I'll only change when I want to."

Firstly, Eric believes in acting upon instinct. Why? Because that is how you act true to yourself. How can you regret an action that is true and honest in your own judgment? To apologise for yourself is either to lie or to admit that your action was not true to yourself in the first place. That kick, for example, was no aberration – in its execution, dramatic style and cause, it was purest Cantona. To apologise for it would be to apologise for one's very existence. Secondly, like Mersault, Eric knows that change to fit the morality of others is both inexcusable and impossible; one's own morality is one's only 'God'. Sorry seems to be the hardest word for good reason...

A great warrior from United's previous glory days, Paddy Crerand, knew the score and led the defence campaign.

"You must understand that if you're a proud man with a keen sense of justice, these moments are hard on you: you're raging inside, you feel sick to the heart and you're bitterly disappointed for yourself and your team. That's something which Sir Matt fully appreciated; that's why I think those people who claimed that Matt would've thrown Eric out were so wrong. Denis, George and me all had our disciplinary troubles and Matt rightly gave us a bollocking and a hefty fine when necessary. But he also knew the position we were in, how difficult referees and opposition players could make it for you. He understood players' temperaments and the pressure of the modern professional game; that's why I know he'd have never shown Eric the door.

"You've still got to be able to look after yourself – nobody else is going to do it for you. Sometimes that'll get you into trouble but there's no alternative.

"It's ironic that Eric has been portrayed as one of football's 'problems'. There is so much to find fault with in the football world: the authorities, referees, the media, our game's technical short-comings...and then there's Eric, who I think is basically a nice, quite shy bloke who just wanted to get on with his profession and be treated fairly."

And few thought Eric was treated fairly during the almost comic coda when the Cantona family sought overseas sanctuary. Officially, this never happened: Eric was alleged to have kung-fu kicked ITN's Terry Lloyd in the chest after being pestered on a Guadaloupe beach and to have thrown in some blood-curdling verbals for good measure. The police turn up, confiscate the film and threaten Lloyd with prosecution for breaching the French-style privacy laws. So far, so funny. But this is the cool bit: within seconds of completing his 'assault', a becalmed Eric turns round, signs an autograph for a fan and starts chatting politely with admiring on-lookers as Lloyd staggers away. Tarantinoesque or what? Like blowing someone's head off as an aside before continuing a discussion of Madonna's hamburger preferences. Eric as a Reservoir Dog, anyone?

Somehow, the entire episode had even augmented Eric's legendary pull with the ladies, according to reports in the women's glossies. Surveying some female Cantonistas for explanations of Eric's eternal sex appeal unearthed the following comments. "He's so dark, deep and brooding – the ultimate macho man"; "He's the bit of rough who can give you a seeing-to then whisper poetry in your ear"; "Strong, silent and masterful – he'd look after you"; "It's the nose, know what I mean?" (?!?); "If he treated you as sensitively as he does the ball, you could have no complaints"; and most root-level of all, "I've heard he's hung like a horse." Well, really, madam; so much for size not mattering.

Naturally, such a standing provokes every kind of sleazy mud-slinging imaginable. Both in France and later at Leeds, rumours have abounded of extra-curricular activity in the Ugandan department. If you believe the ridiculous stories Yorkshire Reds hear in the pubs, you'd conclude that the reason they all shag sheep over there is because Eric had taken all the women. It is said that none of it is true but it still adds a frisson to watching *Men Behaving Badly,* doesn't it? Several Red Devils in this book liked to think they were Ladies' Men – but in truth, George Best is the only competition for Eric. Sorry, Clayton.

But to be serious, what was it that underpinned this extraordinary series of explosions that Cantona called his voyage of life? One pillar, according to Eric himself, is Jean Paul Sartre. Existentialism is the ultimate expression of Kantian autonomy and, in Scruton's phrase, "an imaginative dramatisation of the post-romantic soul"; it is an almost irresistible port of call for any free-spirited voyager whose central concern is individualism, liberty and the usages of freedom – it would be astonishing then if Cantona were not an existentialist. Indeed, it is no fancy to suggest that if Sartre were alive today, he would be a confirmed Cantonista. He has written that the true saint-figure for the modern intellectual is not the hero but the anti-hero who goes through life revealing the moral emptiness of bourgeois conformity – a figure such as Jean Genet who demonstrates that all morals are subjective and that freedom is the right to disobey any law your own morality rejects. Cantona admires Genet hugely; were not his kung-fu kicks, shirt-throwing and Riolaci-baiting precisely the sort of *épater les bourgeois* outrages in which Genet used to specialise?

France's rebel icons are spikey, disconcerting and dangerous. Indeed, our history could be interpreted as a constant battle to keep these Gallic viruses confined to the continent; the fear and loathing that Cantona's arrival inspired in some has a good traditional grounding.

The natural rebelliousness of Eric's French spirit is exacerbated by his personal genetic and environmental inheritance. Ferocious Catalan and Sardinian bloodlines mix at the family's location, the turbulent, anti-capital and anti-capitalist Midi Rouge; add his own self-possessed individualism and spontaneous nature and it is hardly surprising that the code of the Rebel dominates his morality. Look again at his heroes like Jim Morrison, Leo Ferre, Brando and Rimbaud – all outsiders and rebels, sometimes to self-destructive extent. Cantona may well now be a socialist but it is not too fanciful to suggest that had he been of his grand-father's generation, he would have been at home with the POUM anarchist brigades in Barca of whom Orwell wrote so admiringly in *Homage To Catalonia*. In modern Britain, sadly, the spirit, desirability and downright cool of the Rebel died with the miners' hopes in 1984. In the dull, conformist world of Blair and Hague, this facet of Cantona's nature – like so many other elements of his make-up – seems only quaint and old-fashioned to his detractors. Not so, of course, to the Cantonistas, striving to keep old flames burning.

He has at least been a rebel with a cause. There's been the unending struggle against what he sees as illegitimate, corrupt and unjust authority; the constant fight to secure freedom and self-expression in a profession that demands conformity and servility; the refusal to sacrifice his self-respect just in order to please others. Such stands make life more difficult for both himself and those around him but then the suffering of the Rebel was always a greater theme in the literature of rebellion.

There is a further philosophical basis to Eric's credo of instinctive spontaneity. As Cantona has signed up to the Jean Jacques Rousseau concept of the Noble Savage, then it follows that he is driven to allow sentiment, emotion and momentary passion to over-ride any restraints that reason or inhibition would impose. This is precisely the "passion and fire" with which he plays that he concedes "sometimes causes harm"; this is what he meant when he talked of the futility of trying to correct his behavioural instincts – remove the spontaneity which can release both good and bad and you separate the man from his self and his artistic soul. The instinctive, intuitive flash which gives us that Wimbledon volley and the pass to Irwin against Spurs can also result in kung-fu and stamping; it's a sort of Faustian bargain but one which most Red Devils were prepared to accept.

I guess that means those who tried to defend Eric's kung-fu as being "out of character" were either being disingenuous or ignorant. Surely the point was that acting on instinct and being intolerant of attacks on his family are both exactly *in* character. What shocked the English mentality was his failure to keep a stiff upper lip; our phlegmatic character is built on suppressing instinct and maintaining our cool, hence our supposed distaste for hot-blooded and excitable Latin temperaments. As Eric remarked long before Selhurst: "People who accuse me of being disruptive forget I have my reasons – I'm trying to remain as instinctive as possible." I always thought that his stamping on Moncur was far worse than Selhurst Park anyway, being an action which truly did reveal the black edges of the heart. But then not even I would claim his nature is perfect; what does impress is his willingness to allow his spontaneity to reveal the good and bad about him to us. A man who loves his privacy has, in some senses, sacrificed much of it for the greater good of his art. (Sadly, the FA disciplinary committee were never going to buy that as mitigation…)

Cantona contradictions abound; some can be reconciled, some are left unexplained. He is a self-professed existentialist who is nevertheless happily in thrall to his childhood essence. He is a man of cultured artistic temperament who can cast aside the finer sensibilities if a kickin' bundle is in prospect. He is an eternal nomad who still craves the bosom of the family. He engages in prolonged reflective contemplation about life yet acts on a momentary instinct. He is in so many ways quintessentially French yet he rejected that country to live within its opposite. It is an enduring problem for the Cantona student: pick up twenty Eric interviews and you could interpret him twenty different ways. Probably much of it is intentional on his part, like the 60s Mick Jagger whose indefinability drove one critic to remark that he was "weary from chasing his mysterious soul through the mazes of funhouse mirrors he had built to protect it". Indeed, Eric has said, "I don't want to be understood", though you could probably find a quote that says precisely the opposite.

Only the banal and ordinary can be definitively encapsulated in one interpretation. Eric is special. He may be a man of contradiction and mystery but as Walt Whitman once put it with a Cantonesque touch:

I contradict myself?
Very well, then: I contradict myself.
I am large: I contain multitudes.

...and few men in our Red lives loomed as large as Eric Cantona. God Save the King.

BIBLIOGRAPHY

Readers who'd like to dig further into the Red Devil aspect of United's history should find the following as useful as the author has: thanks to the creators of these works, without whom...

Betrayal Of A Legend – Michael Crick and David Smith
The Complete Manchester United Trivia Fact Book – Michael Crick
A Strange Kind Of Glory – Eamon Dunphy
The Pride Of Manchester – Kelly and James
Best: An Intimate Biography – Michael Parkinson
The Good, The Bad and The Bubbly – George Best
Bogotá Bandit – Richard Adamson
Manchester United – Percy Young
The United Alphabet – Garth Dykes
There's Only One United – Geoffrey Green
Always In The Running – Jim White
Call The Doc – Tommy Docherty
Soccer At The Top – Matt Busby
The Manchester United Story – Derek Hodgson
Denis Law: An Autobiography – Denis Law
We Shall Not Be Moved – Lou Macari
Touch And Go – Steve Coppell
Manchester United: My Team – Sammy McIlroy
Alex Stepney – Alex Stepney
Six Years At United – Alex Ferguson
The Black Pearl... – Paul McGrath
Cantona: My Story – Eric Cantona
Cantona Au Paradis/Au Bucher – Patrick Mahé
United: The Legendary Years – Pat Crerand and Denis Law
Football Wizard – John Harding

Plus the author's own works; *The Red Army Years, Cantona* and *United We Stood.*